Pine-Wave Energy™

A GUIDE TO CONFLICT RESOLUTION

Robert James Norton, Ph.D.

Order this book online at www.trafford.com
or email orders@trafford.com

Most Trafford titles are also available at major online book retailers.

© Copyright 2014 Robert James Norton Ph.D.

Cover Design, Layout, and Graphics:
Robert James Norton and Trafford Publishing

Printed in the United States of America.

ISBN: 978-1-4907-4022-5 (sc)
ISBN: 978-1-4907-4023-2 (hc)
ISBN: 978-1-4907-4024-9 (e)

Library of Congress Control Number: 2014911264

While every effort has been made to provide techniques and suggestions toward
conflict resolution, no one can guarantee that they will work for you. We hope,
however, that they will assist you in developing life strategies toward a future
of greater peace. The purpose of this book is to provide insights into conflict
resolution through the perspective of the author. The information provided has
been done so with the clearest of intents with no intention to insult or demean.

Because of the dynamic nature of the Internet, any web addresses or links contained in
this book may have changed since publication and may no longer be valid. The views
expressed in this work are solely those of the author and do not necessarily reflect the
views of the publisher, and the publisher hereby disclaims any responsibility for them.

Trafford rev. 06/25/2014

 www.trafford.com

North America & international
toll-free: 1 888 232 4444 (USA & Canada)
fax: 812 355 4082

A GUIDE TO CONFLICT RESOLUTION

Acknowledgments

I believe that no one becomes truly successful without the support and insight from others. People come into our lives when we need them the most. Without thanking some truly special people who have been instrumental in my journey, I would not be doing justice to this book.

My beautiful wife, Suzette, who has fully supported this endeavor to publish my first book. She is my best friend and forever love. All my students since founding Shoto-Chi, as without them the art would not have developed to become what it is today. My friends inclusive of those on social media that have supported this endeavor. Also, my parents who taught me some extremely valuable life lessons to which I continue to practice. They raised me with the ethics, integrity, and respect to live my life the way I do.

Thank you all!

A GUIDE TO CONFLICT RESOLUTION

Contents

A GUIDE TO CONFLICT RESOLUTION

Foreword

When Rob Norton asked me to write the foreword to his book **"Pine Wave Energy** – A Guide To Conflict Resolution", I only briefly considered saying "No", quickly realizing that we would most likely end up in a scenario of verbal conflict! After reading this book I immediately recognized I would not have had a chance of winning. As Rob points out, "Conflict resolution is about finding a peaceful outcome that suits both or all parties." I can peacefully say that all parties win with this book. Rob has written one of the best books I have ever read on the topic of verbal conflict and resolution and I recommend it to everyone, regardless of their occupation or qualifications

My name is Chris Roberts and I operate SAFE International, a mobile self-defense company operating out of Ontario, Canada. We have taught more than 185,000 women and men of all ages since 1994 and have expanded internationally. I met Rob about one year ago and quickly realized that we shared many of the same philosophies on personal protection. From there a personal and professional relationship grew. We at SAFE International teach verbal conflict resolution with some similar philosophies as Rob, but in this book, Rob has been able to take the reader much further and deeper on conflict resolution than virtually anyone in the self-defense industry.

Our industry is one that generally gives lip service to the topic of verbal conflict resolution. Instructors frequently don't understand the importance of it, don't know how to teach it, or their only solution is teaching to yell "Back Off" at an attacker which has very limited effectiveness. Rob not only gives you many different examples that most can identify with, but he also gives you strategies that can be used immediately, not only in moments of potential violence, but also in our personal lives with loved ones, friends and colleagues.

Rob is the first to admit and recommend that one can and should train for years to improve their effectiveness at conflict resolution. Knowing that most people won't make such a commitment, he does offer many philosophies that can be adopted immediately; from the importance of keeping calm and your emotions out of the conflict, to the Question, Suggestion, and Command (QSC) link that takes place in conflict. He offers many examples that show how our perceptions may be very different from someone else's, and that by listening, understanding, and searching for resolution, the vast majority of conflict can avoid any physical aspect... the perfect end result.

Rob takes you through a chapter on body language, which is the predominant form of communication and its importance in being congruent with the words we use.

If one is looking to learn how to improve their conflict resolution strategies, negotiation skills, or just learn more about themselves, this book is a must read. The topic of conflict resolution is, in my opinion, a much more important step to learn and master than any physical self defense skills that you might learn. Real self-defense is about avoiding physical confrontation and this book will dramatically increase your chances of reaching a peaceful outcome.

Keep SAFE!

Chris Roberts
Managing Director
SAFE International

Introduction

Pine-Wave Energy: A Guide to Conflict Resolution provides a simplistic yet realistic guide to understanding and resolving conflict in normal day-to-day life, with both ourselves and others.

It is a tool to understanding perception within conflict, how emotions become the catalyst for conflict, communication styles, and personality types. It shares effective techniques regarding verbal and nonverbal communication. This is inclusive of the systematically developed QSC strategy for effective verbal communication that can be used in both personal and professional environments.

It is not a book based around combat. Even though it does briefly touch base on the controlling of personal space when there is a perceived or actual physical threat, it is in no way meant as an instruction manual for actual combat. It introduces the basics of the dynamic technique known as the Fence. This technique has been developed over many years of studying human behavioral patterns. This technique integrates NLP (neurolinguistic programming) to assist in the control of one's personal space.

We take a logical approach that provides a proactive guide

aimed at resolving conflict prior to physical engagement, whenever possible.

By reading this book, my goal is for you to gain a greater understanding of conflict resolution, an understanding that we all see things differently, but if we work toward a common goal, then a resolution can be achieved. Most of the contents of this book are aimed at providing you with the knowledge and confidence to look at conflict resolution as something that is obtainable in the best interests of all parties.

After looking into the emotional aspect of conflict, we then look at grasping the concept of perception. This is a fun exercise in understanding the simple concept that we all see things differently. We live different lives through sight, sound, and touch. We experience different things but one thing is for sure—the majority of people on this planet do not enjoy conflict. In many years of studying martial arts and conflict resolution, I know that when I developed Shoto-Chi, it was and still is unique. There are many different arts out there, but most have one thing in common: they deal with conflict from the second a conflict turns physical, either with weapons or without. As we all know, most conflicts do not go physical and the largest form of conflict is that with ourselves. That's right! Ourselves.

By learning effective conflict resolution, you start to put yourself in a better place. The more confident you become in yourself, the better chance you have in resolving conflict with others. Shoto-Chi (a.k.a. Pine-Wave Energy) takes a few steps back from the conventional martial arts world and looks at taking a proactive approach toward resolving conflict by teaching methods of resolution prior to the physical stage whenever possible. This is done so through the understanding of human behavior.

Self-defense is not just about the physical aspect. The largest form of abuse in today's world is emotional. The sad reality of this is that most of that comes from those that are closest to us. Learn to control your emotions, take back the power that you have given to others, and have the attitude to grow, to learn, to adapt, and to become confident in who you are.

Confidence truly is a beautiful thing. It is amazing how many things in life become easier to handle, yet it is experience that brings confidence. The more we do things, the greater the chance we have at becoming better at them; therefore, we develop a greater level of confidence.

As we progress into this book you will hopefully find some insightful and useful skills to adapt into your life. The objective of writing this book is to ask the right questions so that each of you reading it can discover a path toward personal resolution.

What Is Pine-Wave Energy?

Pine-Wave Energy is the English-sounding description of Shoto-Chi. Shoto-Chi is the art developed by founder Robert James Norton in 1990, an art that teaches the realistic approach to conflict resolution through the understanding of human behavior.

The art is uniquely dynamic and teaches how to resolve conflict through strategically developed techniques and philosophies. These techniques have been developed over many years of understanding human behavior within conflict, both physical and especially nonphysical. The art is extremely powerful by teaching the foundations of psychology in order to understand how to effectively read conflict, then manage a suitable resolution in the best interest of all involved parties.

Pine-Wave Energy is also a specifically developed program for focusing children with challenging behaviors. The program integrates the art of Shoto-Chi with additional means of focusing children. This helps to assist them in understanding how their perception of self and others is not getting them the desired results they are truly seeking. Appreciating the need for relaxation is also pivotal to reaching that calmer state.

You will find the relaxation video for Pine-Wave Energy

1

available on YouTube. Here is written content of that video:

Let us begin by sitting in a comfortable position.
Gently allow your eyes to close.

(Best not close your eyes if reading this. LOL!)

Take in a nice deep breath, allowing your stomach to rise.
Now gently open your mouth and slowly breathe out.

As you begin to relax your breathing, start to take note of the
muscles in your body doing the same.
Allow yourself to release any tension.
Allow your muscles to become soft and limp.
Allow that tension to float away, leaving you with a sense of
calmness and tranquility.
Continue throughout the body bringing your entire being to
the same relaxed state of calm.
From your head to your toes you are now feeling relaxed.
Your muscles are starting to feel heavier as they relax.
Your mind is also starting to relax and calm down.

Now fully relaxed, join me on a little journey.

Imagine yourself walking along a trail surrounded by pine
trees. While you're walking, you feel the fallen pines under
your feet. You feel the gentle breeze of the morning air against
your skin. You hear the whispering of the wind through the
trees.

In the distance, you smell the ocean waves gently stroking the shore. You feel inspired to do great things and feel as one with the circulating life energy that surrounds you.

You are completely at peace.

As you continue walking, you come to an opening in the trees. The trail of pines has led you to the beach. You stand still for a moment. You take a nice deep breath in and smell the ocean waves. You remove your shoes and walk barefoot onto the beach. The warm sand under your feet helps you to relax a little more.

You are surrounded with beauty. You feel the life energy around you, and you are at peace with yourself. You feel love for all living things. You are truly inspired by the beauty of life.

Let us now lie down on that warm sand. The gentle breeze continues to brush against your skin. As I count from ten to one, you will slip into a deeper sense of relaxation. A deeper sense of peace. A little deeper with each descending number.

10– 9: Your body starts to mould itself into the sand.
8–7: You release all tension from your brow.
6: You are becoming more relaxed.
5–4: The breeze becomes a little warmer as the sun continues to rise.
3, 2, and 1: You are now deeply relaxed and at peace.

Continue to feel this calmness. You are at peace with yourself. You are seeing things much clearer. Your world becomes clearer and calmer and more relaxed.

In a few moments I shall count to ten. As I do so, you will start to return to an awakened state of peaceful consciousness. You will find it easier to let go of conflict. You will find it easier to love. You will become more energized toward your life.

1, 2, 3: Starting to return.
4–5: Start to move your fingers and toes.
6, 7, 8: Eyes gently open. Eyes gently open!
9–10: You have completely returned; you are awake and aware.

Taking a Positive Approach to Resolving Conflict

A positive attitude works out of opportunity, not obligation. It looks for the best, not the worst, in circumstances. It is can-do, not must-do. It is hopeful, not pessimistic, and a positive attitude can create remarkable results. If you believe as I and many others do that the power of positive thought can change the world we live in, then with this message in your thoughts and heart—go forth and multiply!

Understanding Conflict

Conflict is simply described as a disagreement whereby the involved parties perceive a threat to what is important to them. This could be their needs, interests, or concerns. Within the described definition, there are several methods of understanding conflict. Although conflicts may come in different forms from minor self-choices to major international events, conflicts exist in almost every area of life.

Through many years of understanding and teaching conflict resolution, there has been one question I have always asked: "To whom do we have the largest form of conflict?" The answer that most do not usually initially arrive at yet is the most truthful is our own selves. Indeed, the largest form of conflict is that with our own selves. Every day we may wrestle with a choice. This may be as simple and easy as what to choose for dinner or as hard as whether to remain in an abusive relationship. Life is about making choices. These choices determine our future. These choices are an internal conflict, an internal disagreement.

Our emotions play a huge factor in these conflicts. It is usually our emotional state at the time that dictates if a conflict will even become so. We are emotional beings, and it is the control of these emotions that become an essential tool in resolving conflict.

So let us look at disagreements. Disagreements are a result of a different perspective; therefore, conflict becomes the result. There is a saying that there are usually three sides to every story—mine, yours, and what lies in the middle. The fact is that perception is what makes this statement true. Conflicts are a significant difference in opinion. What may seem like a trivial thing to one is a huge thing to another. Take a type A personality, for example. Most things to them are huge, and it gets them even more irritated when someone with a more laid-back personality doesn't see things in the same way. So is the conflict simply a personality thing or a simple misunderstanding?

It is hard to say as every conflict is different, such as in the subject matter, the people involved, and the environment. There are simply way too many variables to say either way. If those within the conflict can take the time to understand the true nature of the conflict, then there is a possibility to resolve.

As briefly mentioned, we should take into consideration the personalities of those involved. We will go into more depth on personality types later on in this book. How many times have you found yourself in a conflict but seem to be the last person to know? As funny as this sounds, it is more common than you may realize. Quite often we are surprised to find out that someone has an issue with us personally. It may be something that was said, overheard, or seen or the fact that we may simply be guilty by association. The sad reality is that the human race can be extremely judgmental before even finding out the facts. We all have heard the saying "innocent until proven guilty." Unfortunately this is only reality in the legal system. In conflict, people have already made a judgment in their own mind. Therefore, the person is put on the defensive when the accuser brings something to their attention. An even worse situation is when one person within a conflict allows things to fester for a long period before addressing it. This allows the emotional connection to the conflict to deepen and harden, making resolution harder on one or all parties involved.

How a conflict continues is a result of the perceived threat at the time. We tend to respond or react using emotions. These emotions may not be painting the factual picture but rather a fictional one. In order to resolve conflict, we need to calm the perceived threat. Calmness allows us time to think and hopefully respond to that threat in a logical manner with the intention to resolve versus to escalate. Once you are able to reduce the threat to an understanding that there is a conflict, you create an environment of agreement. This can start to lay the groundwork to constructively resolve the conflict in the best interests of all involved.

Upon reaching this stage, we can now start to address their concerns. We need to discover what their concerns are and also what their vested interest is. This is an opportunity to define the conflict to put a name or title to it, so to speak.

Conflict is part of our everyday lives and exists in every relationship. I think it is safe to say that we can't agree upon everything all the time. One of the key skills to resolving conflict is the ability to learn from the conflict. In order to learn from the conflict, we must engage. We must learn how to effectively manage it. Avoidance of conflict will only add to the conflict. As indicated earlier, festering doesn't help in the resolution process. Poor handling of a conflict can cause great hardship to any particular relationship, but good, respectful handling places a positive approach to resolving the conflict. In fact, by learning effective skills to resolve conflict, we learn how to heal wounds and build bridges. These bridges strengthen the connection between the involved parties. Learning effective communication skills to resolve conflict assist us in our personal and professional relationships.

The important thing to remember is that everyone has needs and desires. In order to resolve, we need to get the involved parties to become motivated toward the resolution process. Once those within the conflict have a belief that they will accomplish something that is important to them, they become more open to finding that resolution.

People need to feel that they are being listened to and understood, that their needs are being nurtured, and most of all, that they feel that you can support them in recognizing their concerns. The challenge in all this is that everyone's needs and desires differ. Start by creating the ideal environment that puts those involved in the conflict on neutral ground. Find the common goal, and you have a point of reference to aim toward.

When developing that ideal environment, think of safety. This safety isn't just from possible physical harm but also from emotional. Take the child-versus-parent situation. A child may not have a point of reference of what is dangerous, but through life's experiences, the parent can see the danger way in advance. So as the child tries to experiment or explore, the parent tries to stop them knowing what lies ahead. The child then becomes frustrated, angry, or even possibly enraged when they don't get things their way. The parent achieves their goal of keeping the child safe, but the child doesn't understand that. All they get from the conflict is being told no. In order for that child to learn, they must participate. The child's perception is simple: Mommy or Daddy stopped me from having fun and that's not fair. As parents our job is to teach, to guide, and to love and support. By not allowing our children to experiment or explore can limit their abilities later on in life. The resolution to this is to help the child understand the dangers. Help them to experiment or explore as long as these areas of learning are not a danger to their permanent health. It is good to teach someone how to cross the road safely. It is not so good to teach a child how to get hit by a car!

For us to participate in conflict resolution, especially for the long term, then we must strive toward meeting the needs of all parties to ensure a lasting and equal relationship. Each person within a conflict deserves a respectful conclusion. Even though at times conflicts may seem extremely one-sided, we can make a choice to strive for resolution in the best interests of all parties rather than that of just ourselves. No matter what the relationship, be it with family, friends, or professionals, there is a personal connection. An inability to understand differences results in a disconnect. This disconnect creates conflict. Conflict creates disagreements, arguments, and sometimes physical connection. With all this hostility, you enter the realm of separation. Workplace or corporate structures often produce conflict as there are so many differences of opinions on how things should be done or what is deemed as a priority. It is all good for the president of a company to demand certain things, but if those expected to follow don't truly understand the importance and reasoning, it is hard from them to comprehend why. Better communication toward educating the common goal helps that understanding and team building. This results in better relationships, a happier environment, and most importantly, a compassionate understanding why those that follow are being asked to perform in certain ways. Dictation just adds fuel to an already burning fire.

Understanding the psychology of conflict is also extremely important. In the art of Shoto-Chi we teach by five guiding principal philosophies. They were written in a particular sequence and can take many years to master. Like most things, it is a choice to begin and continue the process. Here we cover the five principal philosophies that are taught within Shoto-Chi.

Principal Philosophy 1:
Remember to keep calm and in control of your emotions.

The first and most difficult to master. Conflict is a result of heightened emotions. For the most part when one person is in a heightened emotional state, those emotions affect the others within the conflict; hence conflicts continue.

Calmness is paramount and one of the most usable skills in almost all aspects of life. It doesn't matter if you are entering conflict or climbing a mountain. Calmness helps us to focus. It allows us to digest information and objectively make a decision. When in conflict with another, calmness provides us structure. It provides us the key skill to attempt to resolve. It allows us to think and to evaluate the conflict, the environment, and the potential impact our actions will have on the conflict. As easy as this sounds, it is not. I'm sure that everyone reading this can think of multiple occasions when one has lost their cool. Multiple times when one has said or done things that they later regretted. Why? Because we allowed our emotions to guide the conflict versus taking a calm and logical approach. There are many methods of calming the mind, but the reality of it is that, within conflict, we quite often do not have the luxury of time to close our eyes and count to ten. Calmness needs to become similar to a light switch. We should be able to turn it on or off as needed. If only it was that simple . . .

There is no doubt that many reading this will think, *Okay then, how does one learn to switch calmness on like a light switch?* Do not be in a hurry. The quicker you force such a dramatic change in your thought process, the least chance you have of learning calmness. It is proven that it takes approximately three months for the human brain to create a habit. This means it takes time of consistent behavior for the brain to start making things more instinctive. Remember, you are learning to resolve conflict. Like most things you learn, it takes time. To begin this process, we must look inside ourselves. Start to really take note of what or who pushes your buttons. What is it specifically that raises the blood pressure? If it is particular person, think what it is about this person. Narrow down the reasons, then start to analyze why you react in the way you do. My suggestion is this: Start a journal. Write down all your interactions not just with people but also with circumstances and environments. Write down the time of day it occurs and what led up to the conflict. As mentioned much earlier in this book, the largest form of conflict is that with our own selves. By keeping a journal, we start to see the patterns within our own behavior. Upon doing so, we can then start to ask that open-ended question of why.

Why do we react in the way we do? Is it a particular time of day or after seeing a particular person? Is it whenever you look at yourself in the mirror or get home from work?

The questions of why helps us to evaluate. But we must be brutally honest with ourselves. It is far too easy to brush off the true reason why we react the way we do. It is far too easy to say "I don't know." If you really want to understand yourself, you must be able to ask yourself the hard questions. In understanding yourself, you can then start the process of effectively understanding others.

The question of why is like peeling the layers of an onion away until you finally reach the core. Every layer you peel away produces another question. It is the most common method used within psychology. Although we can ask the question of others in order to find answers, the most effective use of "why" is when we ask ourselves. It can certainly help to have someone close to you to help guide the process. You are not looking to ask why by itself, but as part of a bigger question.

Q. Why do think you react in that way?
A. Because he makes me so angry.

Q. What is it about him that makes you angry?
A. He thinks he's always right.

People are who they are. If they are unwilling to change or have no consideration for others, then we must develop our own personal skills to not allow their behavior to negatively affect our lives.

Q. Why do you think he behaves this way?
A. He's insecure!

It is quite possibly correct that those that feel the need to constantly be right haven't obtained the life skills to adapt. They are controlling of everything and everyone around them.

Q. Do you think you can adapt?
A. Yes.

Q. Why?
A. Because I like to consider others' thoughts and feelings.

Q. If this is correct, then why do you react this way to him?
A. Because he is close to me and I don't like to be controlled.
I had enough of this growing up.

Now we are getting somewhere. During these guided questions, we have now peeled away a few layers of the onion and are getting closer to understanding why we react the way we do. The more we understand, the calmer we shall eventually become once we learn to let go of the reasons. In order to move on, we need to learn from the past, then let it go. Calmness is a state of inner peace. Inner peace is close to impossible when holding on to something that is perceived as negative in our past. Turn the negative into a positive, and you turn anger into calmness.

Principal Philosophy 2:
Remember, words can never harm you!

This principal philosophy is the most debated of all of them. At first glance, most that are reading this will disagree. Words can harm you, right?

Words revoke an emotional reaction. When we learn to

control these emotions, words no longer have the impact they once did. Similar to learning calmness, this principal philosophy takes time and until calmness is achieved words will continue to cut into our feelings.

Within conflict many are quick to use words as weapons. They lash out while emotionally driven without consideration of the feelings of others. Words can only harm us if we allow them to. It is the emotional reaction to these words that affect us on a physical level through stress. To learn effective conflict resolution, this statement must be viewed in a positive light so not to affect us emotionally or physically. Not only should we not allow words to influence our decision making but we should also never use words to attack others.

Most conflicts are solely of a verbal nature. Very few conflicts turn physical, so it is important that we learn how to effectively resolve verbal-based conflicts. Even when there is a physical element to a conflict, we still have an opportunity to use verbal interaction with the intention to resolve. This may come before, during, or after physical involvement.

In future chapters we will look into verbal conflict and the understanding and importance of the QSC strategy.

With a calm mind, we can resolve many conflicts. Allowing words cutting into our feelings is a choice. At the time of an emotional engagement, it may not seem an easy choice because those very emotions are the catalyst for the conflict continuing. I suggest focusing on calmness before conditioning the mind to shut out words that have an emotional bearing on you. As you will find throughout all the five guiding principal philosophies, once you master calmness, the others will start to become easier to manage.

Principal Philosophy 3:
Read and understand one's body language.

Now onto one of my favorite subjects being that of our nonverbal communications, or body language, as most people refer to it!

This principal philosophy covers understanding all those within the conflict inclusive of ourselves. To effectively read others, we must first understand the signals we are emitting ourselves. Later in this book is the specific chapter dedicated to nonverbal communication. At that time you will learn about nonverbal cues and gestures. Before we reach that chapter, try to become more cognizant of the signals you are emitting. Understand how your emotions play an important factor in these signals. Take note of how people interact with you at different times of day and especially in conjunction with the emotions at the time.

Principal Philosophy 4:
Remember to look and feel confident.

The quote "Confidence is beautiful" becomes an important

aspect within conflict. Similar to the previous principal philosophy, there are two sides to it. Self-confidence helps us in so many ways. It helps us to be calm, knowing we can digest information and act upon logic though confidence versus that of ego. The other aspect is that those we find ourselves in conflict with are able to see we can digest information but also that we have the ability to search for equality within the conflict resolution process. There needs to be confident approach taken to resolving conflict. Sometimes this can be dominant as it does take a degree of assertiveness to get the resolution process started, especially when the other party or parties are unwilling to initially participate in the healing process. The assertiveness through confidence must be there but with the intention to seek a resolute state through equality and not superiority.

Principal Philosophy 5:
Control your fear; don't let it control you.

The premise behind the final philosophy is to understand our own fears within conflict. It is not aimed at taking an egotistical approach by saying "We have no fear," because we all do. It is learning what makes us tick and how to effectively manage all appropriate responses. Remember that there are five principal philosophies. Based upon the order in which they have been written, by this point you would have had a wonderful insight and understanding of the other four. As a result of doing so, the controlling of fear becomes much easier.

You will a find a couple of these philosophies mentioned throughout the book. As such, things will become a little clearer. My reasoning behind sharing these now is so you can focus on the fact that there is much to understand to truly and effectively resolve conflict. This is not a fix-it-all book, but it is a guide to conflict resolution.

Conflict Resolution:
Tip of Day!

For the most part we tend to make those important decisions in the heat of the moment. Those important moments are usually filled with a string of emotions. At that time we may have a tendency to say or do things we may regret. Take a moment and think. Use logic to calm those emotions then make those life defining choices based upon fact.

Emotions within Conflict

Conflict is a result of an emotional response toward a specific subject. One quote I always use while teaching is "There is no truth, only the perception of truth." It is our perception of what is truth in our own mind that dictates our emotional response. In conflict these emotional responses are what initiates frustration, anger and other heightened emotional states.

It is also these heightened emotions in conjunction with the personality type that dictate the nature of the conflict. Someone with a calm approach to conflict will be able to tolerate more, show less emotion, and control their choice of words. However, just because this type of personality is calm on the outside doesn't always reflect what is going on in their mind. The difference is their level of self-control.

Conflict is a result of a difference of opinion, a different perception, a different emotional response, and a different take on what is right. We have touched base already on the ability to resolve conflict means that one person must have the desire to resolve versus continue. Most people within conflict just want to be right, to prove their point, and to disregard the opinion and feelings of those they are in conflict with. It is a little hard to find a peaceful resolution when those within the conflict just have to be right at all costs!

So let's delve into the emotional state within conflict. What make us have an emotional response?

Well, it is our history that allows us to place an emotional response to everything we see, do, and hear. These emotions help guide us through life, but it these very emotions that can create conflict not just with others but also with ourselves. When we look at ourselves, and I mean really look at ourselves, we see just how many conflicts we have in the space of a single day. From the time the alarm goes off in the morning to the time we finally close our eyes and go to sleep, our brain is in constant decision mode. Are these decisions a conflict? They are to some degree, depending upon what the choice happens to be.

The alarm goes off and we hit the snooze button. We then start the decision process of getting out of bed right away or just hanging in there until the snooze alarm goes off again. When we finally crawl out of bed, we think about what clothes to wear. Now this is certainly a lot harder choice for some versus others, but I think you understand a little about the minor conflict we start our day with.

As the day progresses, the decisions become a little harder. They become a little less routine and therefore a little more difficult. Just imagine for a second you decided to press that snooze button one too many times and now you are late for work. You now have to make the choice between breakfast and heading straight out the door. You choose to skip breakfast. It may not be the greatest choice, but most of us have done it. Now, you get in the car and start driving to work. As you get a little way up the street, you realize that you forgot to put gas in the car the previous day. You know you are already late for work and now you are going to be even later!

You stop for gas then notice the tire needs air. Oh yes! The day is going from bad to worse. So you can answer this for yourself. What is now your emotional condition?

When you finally get to work late, your boss calls you into the office. The amount of inner conflict is now far greater than had you made the choice to get up when the original alarm sounded.

That's right! Conflict is a result of our emotional reaction to circumstances. But emotions are a choice. Certainly not an easy choice at times, but by taking just a few second to digest information, we can approach conflict calmer.

Too often we underestimate the power of emotions and the part they play in our decision making. Emotions are the catalyst for conflict. The lightest of touches or a smile from a friend provides an emotional response. Hearing a comforting song or receiving a compliment provides much-needed stimulus. The smallest act of kindness can have the potential to completely shape our day. The same applies to the one word from a loved one chosen to belittle. Our emotional reaction to hearing certain words or receiving certain touches provides us with our emotions. So it is of no surprise that conflicts are result of emotions.

The biggest gift you can ever give someone within conflict, or in life for that matter, is to listen. Listening is simply one of the most sincere forms of respect. In most cases someone just needs you to listen, to understand their reasons for being upset, and to provide support if needed.

When you are able to deal with your emotional reaction to circumstances, you can then start the process of resolving internal conflict. You will begin to heal when you release past hurt, forgive those who have caused you past pain, and most of all, forgive yourself for your own mistakes. Our emotions do indeed come from many sources. Our thoughts and actions are like a boomerang. They come back to us in the form of emotions. Think, speak, and act with intentions of receiving back what you send out. Send out positive thoughts so that your emotions remain clear. Clear your emotions and you put yourself in a wonderful position to work with others within conflict to find a peaceful resolution.

Once you clear your own emotions, you are now in a position to inject logic. But remember, if the conflict is with someone else, then we now need to work through their emotional connection. This can be done in the same way you have done so with yourself. Help them to understand the emotional connection by listening and acknowledging their perception of the conflict. Acknowledgment of feelings is extremely important to building that connection.

To assist that emotional connection within conflict, we must first listen. We must listen to them completely not just the words that may be coming out but more importantly the unspoken words through their body language. We shall be going into greater depth surrounding body language later in this book. The most important thing to remember is to keep our body language positive and open to receiving their emotions. Display facial expressions of interest and calmness. Keep other nonverbal communication cues open and maybe use a reassuring touch if the relationship allows it.

We look to see and hear how they are feeling. What words are they choosing to use? What specific emotions are they expressing?

By listening, and I mean truly listening, we learn not only what we need in order to even think about resolving the conflict but also how we can build that important foundation to which I have already spoken about. When we listen, we connect. We connect to the words and to the emotions behind the words. We connect to the nonverbal signals and what is not being said or at least verbalized.

Now remember, I have also mentioned about resolving our own inner conflicts. By listening to others, we also become stronger in ourselves. When we take the time to listen and understand their conflict and emit positive body language back to them, it opens the gates to them receiving our input at the appropriate time.

Upon listening and building that foundation, we have now laid down some much-needed mutual respect. We have shown them that their emotions, their perceptions of the conflict are valid, that resolving the conflict has become a priority to us, and that we are looking to resolve that conflict in the best interest of the relationship versus just our own needs, providing those within the conflict peace of mind that we are not looking to win the conflict but to resolve.

So now that the foundation is set, it is time to build on top of it. We don't want to revisit the past as this would be like smashing the foundation that has just set. We must focus on the here and now. The past is the past. We cannot change the past, and by living there, we can never move forward. The future hasn't happened yet, so we must focus on the present. Let go of anything in the past that can prevent you from moving forward. The past is there for a reference. It cannot be changed, but it can be learned from.

Our ability to do this helps us and those we are in conflict with on so many levels. For us we are making a positive choice to move on, to take the high road and look toward a brighter future. By doing this we are helping our own emotional well-being. So we focus on the now. We get real with what the conflict is. We don't cloud it over by focusing on the past or the future. We keep it current. What is the nature of the conflict? How does this conflict react with us on an emotional level? We are not looking at passing blame but we are looking to resolve, and understanding the conflict and the emotions within the conflict can make us work toward the solution.

Now we all know that conflicts can be an emotional roller-coaster at times and extremely taxing on those emotions at that. It is our responsibility to self to truly knowing what resolutions are important to us. At times we simply need space. Sometimes that is enough, but quite often it is not as the conflict will arise again if not resolved. So pick wisely and decide which conflicts need to be dealt with at the time or at a later stage. The key to this is reaching that agreement. When a positive mutual agreement can be reached, it is a good sign that conflicts can get resolved.

Do you circle the parking lot at the local mall at holiday time for twenty minutes, waiting for that spot near the entrance or simply park a little further away and take the five-minute walk?

It is a choice, but logic will dictate the answer. If you are planning on buying a BBQ, you want to be close by, but if you are just buying small easy-to-carry items, then get some exercise!

Okay, so we have addressed the need to listen and absorb information; we have covered the importance of keeping things current and working from a solid foundation of mutual respect. Now we must be prepared and willing to find that resolute state. In order to do this we must let go of that burning desire to prove ourselves to be right. We must let go of any negative thoughts and emotions toward that person; otherwise they will create a huge black cloud over the current situation. It is impossible to stay dry under a cloud of pouring rain when you have no umbrella!

To resolve the present state, we must address the emotions of the present state. We therefore look to calm those emotions versus escalating them. Know that in order to do so, we need to let go. As the saying goes, it takes two to tango! Both parties must be willing to seek that resolution. We can help that resolution along, hence the reason for this book, or sometimes that requires us to simply walk away when the other party wants no part of it. We simply agree to disagree.

The last thing I would also like to add in this chapter is the importance of humor. It is a psychological fact that people retain more information when humor is used. This is not saying that conflict resolution should be seen as a joke, but injecting relief into a conflict has huge benefits when dealing with emotion. But a balance must be found. The last thing we want is to attempt to lighten up the conflict by injecting humor at an inappropriate time. It just makes them upset as they feel you are not respecting their current emotional state. There is enough stress in conflict without misreading the situation and adding humor.

Once we bring balance to a conflict through effective listening skills and positive nonverbal communication, then we are in a position to inject humor. Humor releases the tension. It sends signals to the brain that fire up the pleasure regions and changes the emotional state of mind. This helps us to relax and to experience joy and calmness and therefore puts us in a place for resolution.

There have been many studies done regarding humor that have proven the positive effects when facing adversity. We must, however, proceed with caution and not get carried away. Humor will only last so long. It only masks the issues at hand but certainly provides us with a stepping stone to achieving that resolute state. Just remember that, when using humor to assist in resolving conflict, you are carefully cradling someone's emotions. It is of the upmost importance that this is respected and that the laughter is with the other person and not at them. Use it to release the tension, then move on to dealing with the issue at hand. Just because you find something funny doesn't mean that they will in their present emotional condition.

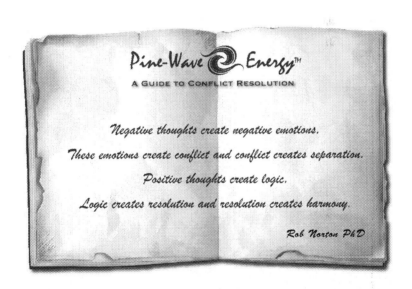

Pine-Wave Energy™
A GUIDE TO CONFLICT RESOLUTION

Negative thoughts create negative emotions.
These emotions create conflict and conflict creates separation.
Positive thoughts create logic.
Logic creates resolution and resolution creates harmony.

Rob Norton PhD

Perception

Conflict is a result of a difference of opinion. We all see things differently. We have a different perception on what is seen to be the truth. It is our emotional relationship to the subject that causes the conflict. These emotions become more intense as those within a conflict continue to have a different perception.

If one sees one color and the other sees something different, then who is correct?

If one sees a glass half-full while the other sees it as half-empty, then who is correct?

Our perception is what makes something true to us. Think of the question concerning color. What if one person was color-blind? Now they are both correct in their own mind.

In order to resolve conflict, we need to understand and respect that others may see or understand things differently to us. When in conflict, think resolution versus continuation of the conflict.

Be patient and understanding. Listen without judgment or prejudice. Remain calm and in control of your emotions.

Above all, never use words to attack others.

Let us start a short journey toward understanding perception. When you look at the images on the following pages, take a few moments to fully understand what you see. What is your perception?

These images have been selected to engage a response. Based upon who we are, our emotional state at the time, and the environment we may be in, our perception may change.

This journey toward understanding perception can be difficult for the simple reason of understanding emotions. It is usually our emotional reaction to what we see or hear that initiates conflict. We may see something we do not agree with or hear something not to our pleasing.

Conflict resolution requires calmness. A calm state creates the opportunity to effectively digest information in such a way that we can make sense of it. We may not always agree with what we see or hear, but one thing is for sure: one or all within the conflict must be calm in order to resolve.

True resolution is aiming to resolve in the best interests of all parties. For example, a physical conflict usually concludes with one person becoming hurt more than the other. However, it is a choice to use excessive force versus the use of necessary force. Although one person may not appreciate the efforts you are making to conclude a physical conflict without the use of excessive force, it is the resolution of our selves that is important from an ethical stand point.

The art of Shoto-Chi (Pine-Wave Energy) teaches direct techniques to resolve physical conflict without the need for excessive force. It specializes in reading people to understand their intent both physical and nonphysical.

In this image we see an eaten apple core with its reflection being that of a fresh untouched apple. At times we all see things we want to see or we hear things we want to hear.

This image represents what we can be when we look into the mirror. Confidence is a beautiful thing. Having the ability to appreciate differences even though we may not agree is open-minded. An open-minded attitude is required.

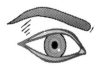 What do you see?

The key to learning effective conflict resolution techniques is understanding that we are see things differently.

Take a close look at the glass.

Some will see this as a glass half-full while others a glass half-empty. Is one right and the other wrong? Well, they are both right. The only difference is that those seeing the glass as half-full have a greater positive approach to life.

If we look at the glass and automatically see both, then it demonstrates that we have the ability to see both sides.

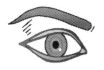 What do you see?

As we take a look at this next image, keep in mind of what has been taught up to this point. We all see things differently.

As in the previous image of the glass, there are two things to see. Some see one thing; others see something else. Like before, there are those that automatically see both, suggesting an ability to see both sides of a conflict.

See what do you see?

You will note in this instance, I didn't provide you with the answer, with good reason!

 What do you see?

Hopefully as we move on to the third image you are now starting to grasp a greater understanding of perception. In this third image, we now come across an illusion whereby a greater percentage of those looking at it see a duck.

Do you see the duck, or was it that I pointed it out?

What else do you see?

 What do you see?

Image 4 brings us close to the end of our little journey into understanding perception. Here we have an image that has two very distinctive figures. Both figures are female but of very different ages.

Can you see the young lady and old woman?

 What do you see?

And now for the final image in this journey. By now you should have a clearer and simpler perspective on the fact that people do see things differently.

There is no truth, only the perception of truth.

So to finish, what is it you see in this picture?

If you don't see it at first, don't worry. It can be a little difficult at first, but once you see it, you will find it hard to forget!

Need a hint?

I'll place the answer at the end of this chapter!

As my quote stated on the previous page,

There is no truth, only the perception of truth.

This is a highly contested quoted and one that I have had many discussions with people over the years. The amusing thing is that this statement itself can cause conflict. You see, the statement is all about perception. To say "there is no truth" is a bold statement to make. However, when you think that everyone perceives things differently, then the truth may change "only the perception of truth." Remember we are talking about a way of recognizing why a conflict exists. By appreciating that everyone doesn't think, hear, feel, or see the same way as you starts a process of resolution.

So why does it start the process of resolution?

Because you have taken the mental approach to accept that we all think, hear, feel, and see things differently. By doing so, it means you have taken time to think, therefore using logic versus an emotional response. Logic has allowed you to slow down. It has allowed you the opportunity to accept not necessarily their understanding of the conflict but simply that they do understand the conflict differently from you. Something else to understand is that the other party may not even think a conflict exists.

Perception
is
the way in which we understand or
interrupt.

41

Let's take a look at some situations that may have occurred at some point in your life. We start by simply outlining the event that has led to the potential conflict.

1. You have parked your car at the grocery store. At the time of parking, there is no car next to yours. By the time you come out, there is an old banged-up car next to yours. The driver has just closed their door as they exited their vehicle. You look at your car and see a dent.

2. You are called into the office of your boss. Upon your entering, he/she starts screaming at you because you failed to get the report to them on time.

3. You left work early. When you arrived home, there was an unfamiliar car on your driveway. You thought your partner was at work.

4. A friend has uploaded a picture of you kissing someone other than your partner. It was a friendly innocent kiss, but photos can be seen in whatever light the person want to see them in. Your partner has also seen the picture. They want answers and are less than pleased.

For now we shall leave these examples just how we started them. You can certainly have some fun with them and act out how you would have responded, but for now I say this: read on and learn more.

More importantly, start to digest what was going through your mind at the time of reading the example. What did you perceive to be the truth at the time? Did you jump to any conclusions? What questions did you ask yourself?

How about we finish this section on a fun note? As we now know, perception is the way in which we understand or interrupt. First, read the word below. What do you read?

LIFEISNOWHERE

Life depends upon the way in which we look at it. Did you initially see the positive or negative statement? They are both there to see. Now isn't that interesting!

So now with a little guidance provided regarding perception, I'm sure you can see how much this plays a part in understanding conflict. To understand a little more, think about breaking it down into a few stages. First, understand how you perceive things. What are your own internal communications?

Are you confident in your perception and are you willing to listen to the opinion of others?

You can certainly go into conflict offering your point of view, but try to refrain from ramming your opinion down the throats of others. Certainly offer your perception, but do so in a constructive manner.

Think back to the color situation at the start of this chapter. Let's say you see red. You know what you see and are 100 percent sure it is red. When someone else indicates that the color is green in their perception of what they see, a conflict may begin.

Moving beyond your own perception, now think about the connection with another. The conflict is the result of a different perception. How you engage and effectively interact with those within the conflict is what will determine the outcome. Have the confidence to allow yourself to hear the perception of another. By doing so, you start to build the trust. Trust is the foundation of relationships. See the conflict as a start of a brand-new relationship. It requires nurturing to grow as does a flower requiring water. Each party needs to build that trust. Listening and understanding that we all have different perceptions helps to build that trust.

As we return to that color conflict, we can start to build that trust by understanding how someone can see green when it is clearly red!

Instead of trying to prove ourselves right by forcing our perception on others, we have now taken the time to calm our thoughts. We have listened without judgment. We have heard that there is a difference in perception. We know in our mind that the color is red, but why does the other person believe it is green ?

Simply by allowing ourselves the freedom to accept that theirs is a different perception allows our mind to ask questions. These questions may not always need to be verbalized, and a little constraint may also be appreciated by the other party.

We have now taken into consideration that this conflict can be resolved because we are willing to see a different perspective. We may not agree upon the outcome but can agree that we all see things differently.

The person within the conflict sees green with the same clarity as the person seeing red. As we have accepted that there are different perceptions at play, we don't look to force the issue but to understand the perception. By doing so, we come to the realization that the other person is color-blind. As a result of being so, they are unable to see reds. Therefore, reds become greens.

So we can now accept that at times both people within the conflict can actually be right because we simply have a different perception of the truth!

We conclude this chapter before people raise the issue of those that murder others and carry out other serious crimes. We are looking at day-to-day conflicts, not serious crimes where it is the legal system's responsibility to pass judgment.

Teaching about perception is about the thought process, not the action. Learning about perception can help you in many areas of life. As we shall touch base on later, body language is the majority of our communication. Perception plays a huge part in this, and understanding the signals we emit helps us to understand the perception of self to some degree.

To address one of the previous perception images. If you couldn't see it. What are we when we are born? That's right. Go back to the image of the tree and water and see if you can find the baby. It's there!

In Order to Resolve, We Need to Be Positive

Today I am a receiver of positive energy. In receiving,
I shall give. I shall choose to conduct that energy like a
symphony orchestra. I shall send out energy to the universe
that touches the hearts of all I come into contact with. I start
here with you. I send you my love and a sense of peace to
have a day filled with joy, happiness, and love that makes
your heart smile. Take this feeling and allow it to manifest
to everyone you touch.

Personalities within Conflict

In the chapter "Understanding Conflict," we indicated the importance of understanding personalities within conflict. So now we take a look at this area.

Among some of the emotions within conflict, there is frustration to which there are three stages: anger, hatred, and rage. Each one of these has a massive impact on how conflicts start, continue, and hopefully resolve. These emotions are in all of us, but it is our personalities that determine how we manage these emotions. For example, take someone with a placid demeanor. When this person becomes frustrated, we may not even see it. However, if someone with a type A personality becomes frustrated (which is kind of easy at the best of times), then it is hard not to notice it.

The same can also be said about the physical aspect. Pushing is a direct result of frustration. As mentioned earlier, there are three stages to frustration. There are also many different levels of intensity when someone is pushing another. Obviously physical strength and control plays a factor, but it is the personality and emotion that dictates the intensity. Do you know, I mean truly know and understand, your own personality? Do you understand what or who pushes your buttons? Do you understand why you react the way in which you do?

So let's look at a few different personalities that may describe you within conflict.

Are you the avoiding type of person that does everything in their power to reduce conflict by not being part of it?

The type of person may still enjoy being around others but also looks for the quickest exit when things become a little heated. This does not resolve the conflict as the parties involved do not have the opportunity to discuss. It just allows for future disconnect. Avoiding the issue at the time when emotions are at their highest is sometimes a good idea, but it must be revisited. It allows for that calming period, but the problem is still there, and not returning to it only allows for the problem to fester.

At the opposite side of the spectrum there are those that do not shy away from conflict. These people want to do what ever is possible to bring parties together. They are the peace makers. They appreciate that everyone has a voice and needs to be heard. They like to mediate if the conflict is between others or if they are involved they will ensure they take the time to listen. They remain calm even when others around them may not be. They enjoy looking for the compromise to ensure both or all parties walk way feeling good about the outcome.

Now there are also those that are naturally volatile. This personality is the volcano waiting to erupt. This personality is certainly described as passionate. They are the louder people in the room. They have enough energy to light the fire and keep it burning all through the night. One thing for sure is that this personality will not shy away from conflict. They thrive on debating in conflict because they have a need to be heard. However, this type of personality believes that in order to obtain balance, then everyone must show their entire hand of cards. This intensity often escalates the conflict as others do not appreciate their approach, but that is what they know. They do also have the ability to show a more loving nature when they put their mind to it.

The most destructive type of personality is those that just have to be right. They have absolutely no regard for the opinion of others. They will use every single opportunity to put the other person down. They won't listen to what others say unless it supports their own train of thought. They will interrupt at every opportunity to ensure they are heard. Their objective is to win at what ever cost. They do not know the meaning of equality. They will start, continue, and end a conflict in their best interests and be damned with everyone else. They are extremely hostile and more than likely suffer from high blood pressure!

Conflict resolution is about finding a peaceful outcome that suits both or all parties. When you have people in conflict with one another that have personalities at the opposite end of the spectrum, then resolution is much harder to come by. This is certainly more prominent when those eruptive types are in conflict with those that do everything in their power to avoid conflict. It is fairly rare, however, to find these personalities in a personal relationship unless the avoiding type wants to be in a controlling relationship with someone that enjoys dominating everything and everyone around them.

So let's take a quick look at the most recognized personality, type A. As described on *Wikipedia*, the theory describes a type A individual as someone who is ambitious, rigidly organized, highly status-conscious, sensitive, truthful, impatient, proactive, and obsessed with time management; always tries to help others; takes on more than they can handle; and wants other people to get to the point. People with type A personalities are often high-achieving workaholics who multitask, push themselves with deadlines, and hate both delays and ambivalence.

In his 1996 book, *Type A Behavior: Its Diagnosis and Treatment,* Friedman suggests that type A behavior is expressed in three major symptoms: free-floating hostility, which can be triggered by even minor incidents; time urgency and impatience, which cause irritation and exasperation usually described as being short-fused; and a competitive drive, which causes stress and an achievement-driven mentality. The first of these symptoms is believed to be covert and therefore less observable, while the other two are more overt.

In addition to type A personalities, it is clear that there must be the opposite. *Wikipedia* continues this by indicating the theory describing type B individuals as a contrast to those with type A personalities. People with type B personality by definition generally live at a lower stress level and typically work steadily, enjoying achievement but not becoming stressed when they do not achieve. When faced with competition, they do not mind losing and either enjoy the game or back down. They may be creative and enjoy exploring ideas and concepts. They are often reflective, thinking about the outer and inner worlds.

Even though type A is one of the most recognizable personalities, there are actually five majorly recognized factors in psychology that determine different personality types. These factors include the following: First, the appreciation of experience creates openness within our approach. There are also the factors surrounding those that plan ahead versus being spontaneous. This is known as conscientiousness. In addition to these factors we also have what's known as extraversion. This involves going out with friends and being energetic. The final two factors are agreeableness and neuroticism, which refer to worrying or being vulnerable.

A good way to determine your personality type is to go within. Take a long and deep look at yourself. Be completely honest while asking the tough questions. When you ask yourself deep, meaningful questions, it is easy to shy away from finding the answers, but it is extremely enlightening. Don't be shy, and ask yourself questions that engage the five factors mentioned herein.

There is also a system known as DISC. This was created by Robert A. Rohm, PhD, and Julie Anne Cross in their book titled You've Got Style. I personally found this to be a truly wonderful insight into personalities. It is a fun and easy read. Certainly this is one I recommend to those of you that would like to learn more about personality profiling without going into huge psychological depth.

The main thing to remember is that we are all different. A combination of personalities is essential to make things happen in life. We all bring something to the table and need to respect these differences in order to start the resolution process. Validating each other in conflict resolution is paramount. This way everyone gets the feeling of equality versus that of being dominated.

Verbal Communication (QSC)

Conflicts come in many forms, but one thing for sure is that they are usually filled with emotional reactions. Emotions are the catalyst for conflict. It is these emotions that drive conflict within us and others.

The art of Shoto-Chi teaches by the five guiding principal philosophies within conflict psychology. The first of which states to "remember to keep calm and in control of your emotions." This is an absolute must. You cannot resolve conflict to the best interest of both or all parties when you are not calm and in control of your own emotions.

The above philosophy can take years to master because, even if we like it or not, we are emotional beings. The philosophy behind the message is to look at the logic behind the emotions. When we are calm, we are in a better place to digest information and come to a logical conclusion. It is this calm state and logical thinking that allows us to start the process of resolving conflict in a peaceful and respectful manner. Emotions usually add fuel to the fire, which escalates conflict because it is hard to think and act calmly when emotions are heightened.

When teaching the art of conflict resolution and especially

the verbal aspect, we break it down into 3 stages. The first of which is "Question."

Question

Why? In order to start the process of resolving conflict, we need to establish the reason behind it. By asking the right questions in the right way, we can start to effectively communicate a resolution. In stating this, it means that the conflict has not started with physical engagement. As you will find out later as we progress into this chapter on verbal communication, there are different stages. Based upon the assessed level of threat, we may need to start at a more assertive stage and circle back. I'll explain more about this as we move forward.

There is a saying that it takes two to tango! One person must be willing to take the initial steps to want to find a resolution, but then both people are required to dance. It is clear to point out the other person is usually the one that is upset to begin with. If both or all parties involved in the conflict are raising their voices or using tones that threaten or deny, then it is extremely difficult to start the healing process. Our nonverbal communication (body language) also plays a huge part in this. Those looking to resolve conflict should emit signals that are calming, open, and certainly nonthreatening. In other words, stay away from big movements, lack of eye contact, crossing of arms or legs, and fidgeting. A calming gesture that can be used in this situations is the called the cupped-hand technique. This emits a calming signal that also helps us to relax.

*The Relaxed
Cupped Hand Technique*

Try to refrain from using a steeple-hand technique as this can be seen as condescending. Keep your hands in sight at all times and your gestures to a minimum.

How do we, or should we, effectively communicate verbally to intentionally resolve a conflict? This is a big question, but question is in fact the answer.

The key to effective verbal conflict resolution is to ask the right questions. We need to uncover the reason for the conflict in order to resolve it. This means to uncover the reason behind the emotion. We do this through effective vocal attributes, such as our tone and pitch. These attributes are paramount as there are many ways to say the same thing. The way in which the message is put across sends subconscious messages to the brain and this is when emotions take over. A simple example of this would be asking "What's up?" If you ask this with calm vocal attributes when someone is emotional, you will obviously get a different reaction from asking them the same thing in a sarcastic undertone. This accounts for approximately 40 percent of communication. Our voice needs to remain calm, nonjudgmental, and nonthreatening and display the intention to resolve.

The words are also essential. The key is to ask what is important to you in order to resolve the conflict, therefore understanding what is important to the other party. We do this by asking open-ended questions. Close-ended questions do not necessarily get us the information we require, so try to stay away from them whenever possible.

Open-ended questions are those that require responses with more than one or two words, such as "How do you suggest we resolve this conflict?" Open-ended questions drive communication, and all the while there is open communication, the chances of a conflict escalating to a physical encounter are reduced—but remember about the key ingredient: calmness!

As I have indicated multiple times over the years, when in conflict, we must simply ask ourselves this: Are we truly looking to resolve the conflict or escalate it? This question may ask the obvious, but when in conflict, it is easy to get pulled into the blame game. Rise above it and keep a calm head. Look toward the result of resolution and ask the questions that get you to this point.

Sometimes, even if we like it or not, the other person or people within a conflict just do not want to listen or find resolution unless they are going to be right. I'm sure most people reading this book can think of someone like that in their lives. This is unfortunate but real. So how do we handle those high-strung personality types that simply want to be right and be damned with everyone else's feelings?

Calmness!—here I said it again!

What does calmness allow us to do?

It allows us to relax, to digest information, to think, to decipher, and to respond calmly. It is also unsettling to those who are deliberately trying to rattle us! When you are calm, less things will rattle your cage. Now, I'm not saying that the words and phrases that others may use to attack won't cut, but by remaining calm, you are in a stronger position to not allow words to harm you (the second of the five guiding principal philosophies of conflict psychology in Shoto-Chi). Think about some recent verbal conflicts that you may have been part of. Hopefully you didn't start them, but even if you did, now is a good chance to learn and understand.

It is a choice to start a conflict as it is a choice to remain in one. One may need space and time to calm down before venturing into resolution. Think about a close relationship whereby that other person didn't like what you just said. You may or may not have intended it in the way it which they perceived it. We cannot fully control how some perceive information as we are not them. We have not lived their lives, and we certainly do not know how they feel. You may have said something to which you thought was innocent or humorous. If the person listening to you wasn't in the right emotional frame of mind to hear what you intended, then they will hear it in a different way, and a conflict begins.

In order to get to the stage of resolution, we need to ask questions. Initially we need to understand where the conflict came from. Did we do something or were we in the wrong place at the wrong time?

In the chapter "Understanding Conflict," we covered that in psychology the same question is asked over and over in slightly different ways. This question is asked until the layers of the onion are peeled back to uncover the underlying issue. That question being "Why?"

By asking this question, we start to get answers. We keep on asking why not as a singular word but as part of a bigger question. The word or question of why, when used as a singular content, will in most cases irritate someone who is already struggling with their emotions. More importantly, ask open-ended questions that show your intent to want to listen, to understand, and to respect their opinion. You may not agree with their perception and reasoning behind the conflict, but you will never be able to resolve a conflict if you make the decision to not listen. People need to be heard. Taking the time to listen means you are taking the time to want to resolve. Listening is the number one skill of effective communication. Asking questions that are seeking resolution versus a continuation through means of targeting shows you have the ability to resolve.

You are searching for answers that will inevitably provide you with the tools to resolve the conflict. Ask the questions when there is time for the person to answer. Display a clean line of sight, ensuring your body language remains open at all times. Be sure to have your feet pointed toward the person (we shall cover body language later in this book). Ask questions with a clear, even, and calm tone. Do not place emotions into your voice. If you feel at the time you are unable to ask the questions without fueling the fire, then attempt to calm yourself. Give yourself a break. This may also help the other person to calm down as well.

who?   **where?**

     what ?

when?   *how?*

     why?

We now move onto the second stage of effective verbal communication (QSC) regarding conflict resolution.

Suggestion

The second stage of verbal conflict introduces suggestion. This is the most difficult to master due to the emotional restraints required. This stage is a natural progression from asking questions. It allows us the opportunity to work toward a peaceful resolution.

Initially this stage is based around equality and not that of authoritative actions. It is carried out with a high level of confidence to show we have the ability and intelligence to search for a resolution within a conflict.

This stage is linked with both Question and the upcoming third stage, Command. When linked with questions, it allows us to work with the other party within the conflict. It brings us to a point where we can ask for their input as to how the conflict can be resolved in their opinion. When linked more with Command, we become more assertive toward the resolution, and therefore we suggest how the conflict can be resolved in our opinion.

Within conflict it is far too easy to go direct to the commanding stage. Learning methods of suggestion when linked to questions is a valuable skill set to have. By learning these skills, it helps us to build a higher tolerance level and therefore a greater level of calmness within conflict.

Using phrases or words such as "Stop" or "Back off" are too aggressive at this stage. Suggestions need to be aimed at resolving the conflict and are supported with open-ended questions. An example of a suggestion linked with a question could be "How do you suggest we resolve this?"

By doing this, we are demonstrating the intention to resolve. By engaging the other party to do so, we are showing a respect toward their opinion. This confuses the mind as they feel unsettled by your calmness when they are attempting to control using emotions. This approach should be demonstrated with calmness and certainly a high level of confidence. The confidence and calmness will send subconscious messages to the mind of the other person. This allows for a greater opportunity at resolving conflict. One of the last things someone is expecting when attacking is for the other person to remain calm then use that calmness to ask for their input. It's not what we say but how we say it.

Most people react upon being attacked (we are not talking about physical attack at this juncture; we shall address this later in the book!). Remaining calm allows us to think. It allows us to address the situation through a logical train of thought versus that of emotions. As previously indicated, this stage is linked to both questions and commands. To understand this in a simple term . . .

Suggestions when linked to questions are open-ended. We ask questions in order to get answers. Through these answers we are able to engage and hopefully discover the root cause of the problem. By doing so we are in a better position to find resolution in the best interest of those involved.

Suggestions when linked to command are much more authoritative. This is introduced once the other link has broken down. At this stage we must now take charge in order to resolve the conflict. We therefore use a greater commanding presence to make the suggestions versus asking for their suggestions. The example of this would be "I suggest we take some time to think about things. When you are ready, let me know." What we have now done is demonstrated a higher level of confidence to take charge but not to excessively dominate. This method of communicating still allows the other person to retreat with dignity, knowing that the issue will still be addressed and hopefully resolved at a later stage.

As we move onto the next stage, Command, we start to look deeper into the authoritative approach sometimes needed to resolve a conflict. This stage is obviously extremely combative. At this point the parties involved are both looking to end the conflict, but the biggest thing to remember is that the other party is only looking to resolve on their terms. We have the ability to remain calm at this stage, and that is critical. As you have previously read, emotions create conflict and logic creates resolution. This is not stating that we should be void of all emotions. It is simply stating that we understand the power of emotions within conflict and that those heightened emotions do not usually serve us well in the resolution process.

Returning to this section on suggestion, here is an example of how a conversation could go when someone's perception is different from reality. This example demonstrates that by remaining calm upon being accused and asking the right questions could result in resolution.

To set the stage for this example, imagine yourself parking

your car in the parking lot of your local grocery store. As you have done many times before, you simply park your car and get out. You then head toward the store. However, at this time, the owner of the vehicle parked next to yours is returning to their car. As they arrive, they notice a dent on their door.

Right away this person becomes angry. Having seen you park next to them and now walking away, they automatically assume you are to blame and become vocal.

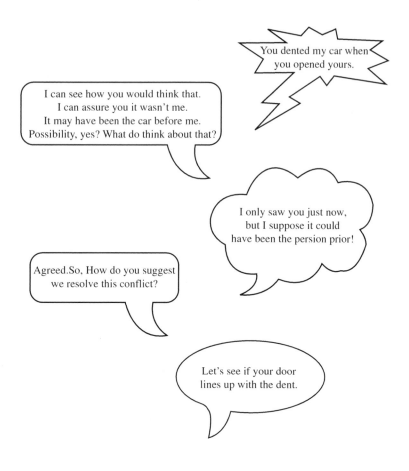

So with some calmness, an open approach to resolving and a positive attitude, things can be resolved.

Obviously every situation is different. The people, emotions, and environment all play important factors. Had the person that was being accused gone on the defensive, then things would have turned out a lot differently. Now, that's not to say that when being accused of something we didn't do, we have the right to go on the defensive. It is simply pointing out that approaching things with calmness changes the dynamics of a conflict. It also helps to keep our stress levels down!

Taking it one stage further, we have now resolved a conflict without the physical aspect. We have also helped someone who is having a rough day to calm down.

Now, the important thing for us to now do is give ourselves a little pat on the back! We have taken the high road and used our integrity. What we shouldn't do is walk away calling the other person all the names under the sun. As tempting as that may be, it only helps in raising the blood pressure. Okay, maybe a little chuckle to ourselves is okay!

We now progress to the most combative stage of verbal communication. As I mentioned earlier while discussing Question, some conflicts may start with more intensity than others. An example of this would be a conflict starting physically.

Command

This is the third stage of verbal conflict. Upon asking questions, asking for suggestions, and possibly offering a suggestion, we enter the most volatile stage of resolving conflict verbally.

At this stage our confidence must be completely shining through. We must be showing confidence but also feeling confident. At this stage we are taking charge by communicating that their behavior is not acceptable and that we are no longer looking for their negative input but looking to resolve the conflict—now.

But once again I must remind you that calmness is the key to success within resolution.

The final stage of verbal conflict can also refer to our perception of a possible pending assault to our physical well-being or from an actual physical attack. Due to that perceived physical threat, our adrenaline puts us into a heightened state. Should this feeling or need to protect ourselves from physical assault arise, then techniques, such as the Fence used in Shoto-Chi, help to control our personal space. It also provides us with a technique to minimize the target area available to the aggressor. In turn this provides us with a small comfort zone and sends out strong nonverbal signals that we shall not tolerate our space being intruded upon.

An authoritative context must now be introduced to relay the message of the intention to resolve with authority. *But be ready!*

Authoritative terminology can also bring about rebellion as aggressive personalities do not like others taking control. In stating this, they may also respect it as you are mirroring part of their own personality. The common statement for this is

We look for in others what we see in ourselves.

It goes without saying that the nonverbal aspect of the

communication must also be authoritative in order to support the verbal message. Words and phrases such as "Stop," "Back off," "Step back," "Back down," and "Walk away" are all authoritative as long as a firm tone is used. Alternative phrasing may include "Seriously!" "Not a good move," or "I seriously do not recommend you take this physical." Such alternative phrasing displays calmness and confidence. It also starts the thought pattern of pointing out that we all make our own choices. As previously mentioned, one must be ready for what could happen next. There are many philosophies surrounding verbal conflict. Many will state that one should never threaten an attacker or tell them what to do. For the most part this is absolutely correct. These tactics should never be used in conjunction with the first two stages, Question and Suggestion. They are simply too aggressive or authoritative for that level of conflict and will easily intensify the conflict when one is searching for resolution.

Giving a choice and providing options pass the ownership to the aggressor. They must then choose fight or flight, knowing that they run the risk of pursuing a physical conflict with someone that has a higher level of intelligence and skill set than they may not have originally anticipated.

Here are a few things to keeps in mind with regards to verbal conflict when there is a high chance of physical assault. Here is a reminder of the five psychological philosophies that Shoto-Chi teaches by. They were written in a specific order and are taught in a specific way. Even though these philosophies are taught over many years of training within the art of Shoto-Chi, they are still a good resource for you.

**Remember to keep calm and
in control of your emotions.**

Remember, words can never harm you.

Read and understand one's body language.

Remember to look and feel confident.

Control your fear; don't let it control you.

Never use words or phrases such as "Please" or "Thank you." These words offer too much respect.

Never repeat yourself—this demonstrates the inability to follow through.

Remember, for a conflict to turn physical, they need to start it. This is not stating that they have to throw the first strike. It is stating that the aggressor has demonstrated intentions of bringing harm to your physical well-being. Within most countries' criminal codes on self-defense, it does indicate that we have the right to strike first if and only if we perceive a threat to our physical well-being and that we have attempted to resolve the conflict through calmer means whenever possible.

At times, conflicts may start at the physical level. At this time we attempt to defend ourselves the best way we know how. Should we be in a position to communicate upon an initial assault, we would more than likely go straight to a heightened adrenaline state and therefore start to state commands to the other person. This is fine. Just because a conflict starts at such an aggressive stage doesn't mean that a resolution cannot still be found. Here the chain that was introduced to you earlier on while discussing the Suggestion stage. Now the chain link is continued and joined to create a circle. As you can see by linking the chain, the three stages of Question, Suggestion, and Command now become linked. Therefore, even with a conflict starting from the Command stage, it can still revert to Question and Suggestion in order to find that resolution.

Question, Suggestion & Command

system works, you can revisit the other stages again to fully comprehend how they all merge together.

When a conflict starts physical, most people will automatically engage with assertive verbal and nonverbal behavior. Emotions are the cause for this, and it is easy to understand why. We have been threatened. As a result of this, we go into a defensive/attack mode. As previously mentioned, not all conflicts start physical. This doesn't mean that the situation or conflict is any more or less intense. The intensity of the threat comes down to how we perceive that threat. How we perceive that threat is largely a result of our emotional state at the time of the conflict. If we calm upon being attacked, there is a larger chance that we will react calmer toward the threat, especially if the threat is nonphysical in nature. Even if the threat is physical, a calm demeanor will certainly handle the situation differently from someone already in a heightened emotional state going in.

For most people Command comes extremely naturally as during our lives we have had to face much adversity, and no doubt we have been put on the defensive on more occasions than we can count. Therefore, when attacked, we go into an automatic defensive mode. There certainly isn't anything wrong with this as we all have the right to defend ourselves based upon the perceived or actual level of threat. In order to resolve conflict, and that is what we are aiming for, one must be able to find their way back to a place where resolution is possible. Let's face it, when both or all parties involved in a conflict are both on the defensive as a result of the push-and-shove scenario, then no one has the intention to resolve.

Allow me to play out a simple scenario for you.

It is Friday night on a cold January evening. Jayne has been working double shifts for the past month in an attempt to bring in some much-needed income. She is tired. Her mind is closing down, and she is in desperate need of a nice long soak in the tub. She clocks out from work at 7:00 p.m. and now has to drive an hour home, knowing full well that she will be stuck in traffic with people on the road that simply do not know how to drive in winter conditions.

Put yourself in her shoes for a moment and try to imagine what is going on inside.

Meanwhile, her husband John is at home. He is out of work and losing all confidence in his abilities to provide for his family. He has become his worst nightmare. He is Mr. Dad!

As a result of their present situation, both are learning to switch roles, but it is not easy to change those daily routines we all become accustomed to.

John has been fighting depression and has a cold. He is also looking after their two-year-old daughter, Sally, who is constantly requiring his attention and craving for her mommy. Even though he is trying to look for work, he cannot focus on the task due to the constant interruptions from Sally. He is doing the housework, the cooking, and the odd jobs around the house. He doesn't have the motherly touch, but he is certainly trying his best as is his wife, Jayne. So let me take a brief recess from this story. Are you taking sides? Or are you having empathy for all involved? Now remember, I haven't even touched base on the emotional state of Sally! She is obviously going to act differently around her dad. Now we have a three-way conflict. It would be easy to fix this story and suddenly say John found a great job and returned to work. Jayne was able to leave her double-shift job and stay at home with their daughter, Sally, but let's face reality, shall we, and look at what is.

We have major personal conflicts going on, and if you remember me stating that the largest form of conflict is with ourselves. Not only do we have those personal, inner conflicts, we also have that tension between the couple. We now continue the story knowing that John and Jayne have not spoken to each other since early morning.

Jayne arrives home after 9:00 p.m. and is utterly exhausted. In the deep recesses of her mind, she is hoping that John has a deep relaxing bath waiting for her after spending the day at home, not really doing too much!

John is upset as he had dinner cooked over an hour ago. As soon as Jayne walks through the door, they both let loose with the problems of the day. This conflict just escalated to an unprecedented level.

As mentioned earlier, the level of the conflict is determined by the emotional state at the time. For this conflict to now be resolved either John or Jayne needs to start the process. Are we at the Question, Suggestion, or Command stage?
Without doubt we find ourselves at command due to the

heightened state. It is not physical, but it is intense. So based upon everything you have now learned, what is the next step? Put yourself into either John's or Jayne's shoes, and think what now needs to happen.

In this case they are both tired. John is upset and shouting at Jayne about dinner being ready over an hour ago. Jayne is upset and shouting that he is not appreciating her efforts, and at the end of a long day, he could at least make her homecoming pleasant. Neither is taking into consideration each other's hardships, both are at a heightened emotional state, but as indicated earlier one must take the initial steps to resolve.

Jayne decides to take the high road. She apologizes to her husband for not calling earlier to let him know that she will be later than expected due to traffic. After doing so, she states that she is going to cool down by taking a nice relaxing bath, and then they can discuss the present conflict. John agrees and does the dishes.

Just by one party taking the initiative to calm down and provide some much-needed space, the conflict has temporarily cooled. Jayne accepted the part she played in the conflict and in turn was able to bring about the possibility of resolution. This conflict has now deescalated from Command to Questions. As previously mentioned and explained in the chain diagram, all three stages are linked together, and by doing so, the possibility of finding resolve even when it is extremely intense becomes a possibility. The QSC strategy was created to not only resolve conflict but to truly understand the dynamics of verbal conflict. It is not easy by any means when implemented into a real-life conflict. Everyone can read and understand and attempt to adopt this strategy, but implementing it when those emotions are heightened is something else.

Role-playing certainly helps, and just like learning realistic self-defense, emotions must be included. The brain reacts completely different under duress, and training the mind to calm is essential. A calm focused mind can create great things. It is also good for our own personal well-being.

Conflict Resolution:
Tip of Day!

Ask questions to find out the nature of the conflict, then integrate suggestions. This is where most conflicts either become resolved or escalated. Ask for their suggestions on how to resolve the conflict. Now combine questions with suggestions to find the resolution. Remember to seek resolution and not a continuation.

Nonverbal Communication

Most of us know that the largest percentage of our communication with others is nonverbal. Body language is nonverbal communication by means of subconscious gestures, movements, and physical attitudes.

It is the signals that are given out to others in the way we act and respond. Be that when we walk down the street or interact with someone. Our emotions play a huge part in our nonverbal communication, and depending upon our personalities, some will emit more signals than others. Think about the emotional states of depression versus anger. Depression will display much smaller movements than anger.

Albert Mehrabian, a pioneer researcher of body language in the 1950s, found that the total impact of a message is about 7 percent verbal (words only) and 38 percent vocal attributes, such as tone, inflections, and other sounds. The other 55 percent of communication is nonverbal. Therefore, 93 percent of communication is in how we say it.

Anthropologist Ray Birdwhistell states that the verbal component of a face-to-face conversation is less than 35 percent. Therefore, over 65 percent of communication is nonverbal.

Research indicates that nonverbal signals carry about five times as much impact as the verbal. When the two are incongruent, it has also been noted that people, especially women, rely on the nonverbal message and disregard the verbal content. Body language generally becomes less pronounced as we get older. It has also been discovered through study of the subject that body language also becomes less pronounced when a person has a higher level of education.

It has been noted through study that a greater level of body language is released when someone is under the influence of alcohol. Most people are unaware of the signals they give out and then wonder why people react to them in the way they do. Body language does certainly change from person to person, but there are common traits to look for.

Toward the start of this book we covered perception. In understanding body language, we must also understand the impact our body language has in the area of perception. We may think we are sending out certain signals, but others may see something completely different. In many cases the way we see ourselves is different from how others actually see us. Perception is therefore being able to spot the contradictions between someone's verbal and nonverbal messages.

Although body language is taught, most is simply picked up throughout our lives. Where the learning comes in are those smaller gestures that quite often pass us by. In order to study and learn body language, we need to realize it is about building patterns. One of the most common debates regarding body language is the perception of someone crossing their arms. Is it defensive?

Think about this. If you start a conversation with someone and they have their arms relaxed at their side, but during the conversation that person suddenly crosses their arms, they are more than likely going on the defensive. But remember, before passing judgment, think about patterns. There was more than likely another signal that supported the defensive behavior. Now if someone already had their arms crossed when you approached them and started the conversation, are they still being defensive? Or what about that same person standing outside in the cold with their arms crossed. Still defensive? The answer is yes. That person may be cold, but they are still being defensive against the elements.

The higher the elevation of the crossed arms and the firmness against the chest indicates the level of nervousness, negativity, hostility, and defensiveness. Add the possibility of clenched fists and now things intensify even further. When someone crosses their arms and grabs the tops of their arms this is a sign of insecurity. Should their thumbs be displayed in an upward position this demonstrates that the person believes themselves to be in control and has that "cool" factor about them!

The more you can read patterns in nonverbal communication, the better. When we move into the next chapter on the three stages of conflict, we will start to cover the controlling of personal space. The technique taught has a specific approach and integrates NLP (neurolinguistic programming). This approach integrates the effective use of verbal and nonverbal communication to engage with the mind of that it is being used against.

But for now let's get back to nonverbal communication and more specifically the actual signals/gestures. To start with, let's look at self-defense. It is important we emit signals of awareness. Awareness is a great deterrent to possible aggressors as aggressors do not want to be caught. If they see you are aware of your surroundings, then they are less likely to take you by surprise. This doesn't make for an easy prey, and that could be good for you.

The third philosophy in conflict resolution within Shoto-Chi is "Read and understand one's body language." This philosophy covers both them and us. Understanding the signals that we and others emit within conflict changes the very dynamic of conflict. It's not that great to just be able to read others if you have no comprehension of how your own body language is interacting with them.

Here are some tips for effectively reading nonverbal cues:

Read gestures in clusters: Each gesture is like a single word and one word may have several different meanings. Gestures come in sentences called clusters. These clusters reveal a person's feelings or attitudes.

Look for congruence: This means that the verbal and

nonverbal messages match each other.

Read gestures in context: Gestures should be considered in the context in which they occur. For example, someone closing off their body language while out in the cold doesn't mean they are being defensive against you. They are simply trying to keep warm and therefore being defensive against the elements.

So while out in the public eye and being aware, remember to display confidence and more importantly be in a position to read others. We should be sending out signals that inform others that we are aware, confident, and in control. Know where you are going and you will be difficult to take by surprise. Walk—aware, briskly, and with purpose—and don't display vulnerability.

Now for me to simply say "display confidence" to those that have a lack of confidence is not helping in the slightest. This is actually one of the most common problems today with some that claim to teach body language. They use the subject of body language but don't actually teach the nuances of nonverbal communication. Well, I am about to give you those dynamics. We shall take some time to look at specific signals within body language surrounding some of the most common emotional conditions within conflict. And remember in conjunction with what you learn in this chapter, we shall also be taking things one step further regarding the dynamic technique know as the Fence, which is used for the controlling of personal space.

Here are some well-known characteristics associated with body language. Remember that recognizing patterns within human behavior is to truly study body language. Someone who is confident will emit different signals to those who are shy, but identifying patterns is the key to reading body language. You have to look at different aspects of someone's personality to produce a good understanding of them. In other words, do not judge someone by a single action.

Always take in account the environment and particular situation when reading a person's body language. Everything is not always as it seems. For example, a soft handshake from a man doesn't, necessarily mean someone of weak character. A person's health condition, such as the presence of disabilities, stress, or fatigue, play an important factor as does a person's profession. So patterns are extremely important. For example, when you see a sudden change in someone's behavior, look for the signs that could include those previously mentioned. Obviously, drugs and alcohol play their part where body language is concerned. Cultural influences also play a huge factor in someone's body language.

Some of the characteristics on the following pages may be listed under more than one heading. Once again, body language is all about recognizing and building patterns, not individual movements. Medical conditions also play an important factor in the emission of body language.

So let's start with what many people are interested in learning about—dishonesty. This is certainly an interesting area to understand within nonverbal communication. There are many that try their hardest to hide their deceit. Some are extremely good at it while others are poor. In most cases those that go out of their way to hide deceit usually give it away in other ways. That is why we say it is about building patterns.

Dishonesty: *(a lack of honesty, esp. a willingness to cheat, steal, lie, or act fraudulently)*
- Playing with the ear
- Shifty or wandering eyes
- Any type of fidgeting
- Rapid speech
- Change in vocal tone
- Shifting back and forth on one's feet or in a chair
- Scratching the side of the nose or neck
- An exaggerated version of the "sincere, furrowed brow" look
- Sweating
- Any activity that obscures the eyes, face, or mouth, such as putting the hand over the mouth while talking, rubbing the nose, or blinking the eyes
- Licking of the lips
- Running the tongue over the teeth
- Leaning forward
- Inappropriate familiarity, such as backslapping, overtouching, and getting too close (invading personal space)

Attentiveness: *(concentrating; paying attention)*
Pensiveness: *(deep in thought / sorrowfully thoughtful)*

- Maintaining strong eye contact
- Gazing steadily at an object
- General stillness
- Tilting or cocking of the head
- Chewing the lips or pencil for an example
- Furrowing of the brow
- Folding the arms and staring into space
- Leaning back in a chair
- Looking upward
- Scratching of the head
- Holding their head in their hands
- Resting their chin on the hands or fingers

Boredom: *(the state of being bored)*
- Wandering eyes
- Gazing into the distance
- Glancing at different objects
- Sighing heavily
- Yawning
- Crossing and uncrossing legs and arms
- Tapping fingers or feet or twiddling of thumbs
- Fiddling with objects
- Doodling
- Pointing the body away from the other person
- Shifting of weight
- Leaning forward and backward in a chair
- Moving one's head from side to side
- Rolling the eyes
- Stretching
- Cradling the chin in the hands while glancing around the room

- Picking at the fingernails or clothing
- Attempting to do another task
- Pointing their feet toward an exit

Frustration (confrontational): *(frustrated; discontented being unable to achieve one's desire)*
- Frequent direct eye contact
- Uttering repetitive phrases
- Closeness to the other person, frequently within their personal space
- Gesturing with the hands
- Pointing
- Shrugging

Frustration *(early stages of surrender):* *(frustrated; discontented being unable to achieve one's desire)*
- Sighs
- Rapid exhaling
- Grimacing
- Hands on the hips
- Hands on the head (in exasperation)
- Exaggerated or melodramatic movements

Frustration *(total surrender):* *(frustrated; discontented being unable to achieve one's desire)*
- Rolling the eyes or closing them
- Shaking the head
- Throwing the hands in the air
- Shrugging
- Turning and walking away

Anger: *(extreme or passionate displeasure; make angry / enrage)*

Hostility: *(being hostile, an enmity, or in a state of warfare)*
• Redness in the face
• Arms, legs, or ankles being crossed
• Hands on the hips
• Short and rapid breath
• Frequent repetition of certain phrases
• Pointing of fingers
• Rapid speech or body motions
• Tenseness
• Locked jaw
• Tightly closed lips
• Frozen expression or scowl
• Stiff, ridged posture
• Shaking
• Fists clenching
• Frustrated, almost uncontrollable arm movements
• False or sarcastic laughter

Depression: *(Psych. a state of extreme dejection or morbidly excessive melancholy; a mood of hopelessness and feelings of inadequacy, often with physical symptoms, such as loss of appetite, insomnia, etc.)*
• Isolation and avoidance of social contact
• Poor concentration
• Inability to focus or plan ahead
• Low and quite speech
• Relaxed, slackened body
• Downcast eyes
• Slow and deliberate movements

- Change in appetite (some quit eating; others overeat)
- Inattention to person hygiene and dress
- Forgetfulness

Grief: *(deep or intense sorrow or mourning)*
Sorrow: *(mental distress caused by bereavement, suffering, or disappointment; grief)*
- Tears
- Listlessness
- Inability to complete normal daily tasks
- Isolation
- Apathy
- Downcast eyes
- Signs of depression and confusion
- Relaxed facial muscles
- Slumped or slackened body
- Motionlessness, or slow and deliberate motion

Indecision: *(lack of decision; hesitation)*
- Shifting back and forth in a chair
- Looking back and forth between two fixed objects
- Tilting head from side to side
- Opening and closing hands, or moving one hand, then the other
- Opening and closing of the mouth without saying anything

Nervousness: *(being worried, anxious, timid, reluctant, afraid, resulting from or reflecting those feelings)*
- Eyes darting back and forth
- Tensing of the body
- Contraction of the body (curling up)

- Shifting of weight from side to side
- Rocking in a chair
- Crossing and uncrossing the arms and legs
- Tapping hands, fingers or feet
- Adjusting or fiddling with pens, cups, eyeglasses, jewelry, clothing, fingernails, hair, hands, etc.
- Wringing the hands
- Clearing of the throat
- Coughing nervously
- Smiling nervously (nervous people often smile, then resume a normal expression, over and over, very quickly)
- Biting of the lips
- Looking downward
- Chattering nervously
- Shaking or quaking (in extreme situations)
- Sweating (in extreme situations)
- Chewing nails or picking cuticles
- Putting hands in pockets
- Rotating side to side with the upper body
- Becoming silent

Now the thing about learning body language is that like any other subject, it needs to be practiced. You have spent your entire life skimming over a fascinating subject and now you get to study in-depth. I must warn you, it can be a lot of fun learning about this subject.

In order to do so, think small at first. If you try to look at all areas at once, it will be difficult to absorb that amount of information. Choose a specific area of the body or a particular emotional state. Focus on that and stay on it until you feel comfortable, then move on. The important thing to remember, though, is to not stare. This obviously makes people feel uncomfortable as does telling them you are reading them. I do admit it that this is something I enjoy doing, especially when having meetings with those trying to sell me something!

Having the ability to read people when they are lying to you is a wonderful skill to have.

As we come close to the end of this chapter, I thought it would be nice to add in a few extra things. The smile can tell us a lot about someone. At times these smiles can be genuine and other times extremely fake. So how can we tell them apart?

The major difference is that a natural smile produces characteristic wrinkles around the eyes. Insincere people smile only with their mouth. We have heard people say that others light up the room when they smile. The reason is the positive emotions displayed through the eyes. It has been proven that, the more you smile, the more positive reactions others will give you. Let's break down the two kinds of smiles into the five most common types:

TIGHT-LIPPED:
The lips form a straight line with the teeth concealed. This indicates the person is usually with holding an opinion or attitude. It can also demonstrate someone who is embarrassed by their dental features.

TWISTED:
One side of the lips with the corresponding eyebrow is raised. The lips are kept tight. This indicates sarcasm.

DROP-JAW:
This opened-mouth smile gives the impression of laughter and playfulness. This indicates a person who is attempting to invoke happy reactions in others.

SIDEWAYS LOOKING UP:
The head is slightly turned away while the eyes seek out the intended target. This indicates a level of shyness but can also come across as a "come on" signal by the opposite sex.

THE GRIN/SMIRK:
The lips are kept together to produce a practical smile. The grin/smirk acknowledges something that is found to be amusing and can also be associated with sarcasm.

I could continue on this subject for a long time and talk about handshakes, geography of the face, stances, additional arm signals, and the list goes on. Nonverbal communication is an absolute passion of mine and something I have studied for many years. I will, however, finish up this chapter by briefly touching base on the eyes—the windows to the soul, as they are commonly known. There is so much to learn from studying the eyes. As detailed as we could go into it, we shall keep it fairly short.

The pupils dilate upon an emotional reaction. Drugs and alcohol can also play a factor in this as does problem solving.

Upon a positive emotional engagement, the pupils can dilate up to four times their normal size. They also contract upon negative emotional reactions.

Men have a higher degree of tunnel vision than women. As a result of this men have a higher ability to see directly in front of them and targeting at long distances. Women have a far superior form of peripheral vision over men, which allows them to see things to around 45 angle mark. Now these skills can be trained and are done so for people working in fields that require excellent awareness.

The eyes do indeed tell us a lot. They are not a 100 percent tell, but in conjunction with other gestures, patterns can be built for a greater accuracy in the read. There are particular regions within the human brain that dictate behavior patterns. These patterns also indicate how the eyes may position themselves through subconscious movements. When the mind focuses, the senses are engaged. As a result the eyes move toward specific regions. Eyes moving up are typical in memory and creative thinking, to the side in hearing, and down in recall or emotions. The head may also move in conjunction with the eyes, such as up to their right for memory. Keep in mind that noticing these gestures requires a trained mind. Most of these movements happen in the blink of an eye. Here is a quick reference guide when looking at someone's face:

Remember this guide is based upon the direction their eyes move, not the mirror version of what we see.

Their top right: Creative thinking or deceit

Their top left: Memory recall

Their sides: Sound recall

Their bottom right: Emotional recall

Their bottom Left: Talking to oneself

The Three Stages of Physical Conflict

In conjunction with the three-stage QSC strategy of verbal conflict being Question, Suggestion, and Command, there are three stages to physical conflict. This chapter briefly explains the concept as taught with the art of Shoto-Chi, but is in no means meant as an instructional guide. This concept is taught over many years within the art and is taught along side the psychological aspect of conflict, verbal and nonverbal communication techniques.

No two conflicts are the same. They vary in how they begin, develop and conclude. Many different factors also come in to the equation, such as personalities, emotional states, and the environment. Only a small percentage of conflicts turn into physical confrontations. In most cases they can and should be avoided with the correct use of verbal and nonverbal communication. As the person on the receiving end of someone's outburst, we have a responsibility to our own well-being. Our priority is to make ourselves feel more comfortable within that confrontational situation and to bring it to a swift conclusion wherever and whenever possible. Here we study the three stages of conflict from a defendant's perspective. Each stage is broken down to describe the emotional, psychological, and physical aspect.

STAGE 1

This is the starting point of the conflict. It describes a change in our environment. Something needs to have happened from the aggressor toward the defendant. This could be afar or up close. Our awareness to the situation and environment is what will dictate this element. In most cases there is a verbal interaction of some kind in conjunction with body language. It could be a deliberate attempt to bait into a physical encounter or simply to put a point across. Conflicts cover all areas of our lives from personal interactions to that in our professional lives. The responsibility of the defendant is to take charge of the situation and make themselves feel more comfortable. By taking charge, this doesn't mean being aggressive but taking the lead to find a resolution to the conflict. The verbal and nonverbal communication messages have to emit confidence and authority.

During this stage there may be a perceived physical threat, but this is down to the senses of the individual. The thirty-second rule of conflict indicates that, if a conflict is to turn physical, it will do so within the first thirty seconds. This is unless we as the defendants change the dynamic of the situation through the improper use of verbal and nonverbal communication.

If we marry up the three stages of verbal conflict, then we are at the Question stage within stage 1 of physical conflict. This means we have the time to ask questions, to get insight as to the reasoning behind the conflict, and therefore to be in a strong position to resolve.

As previously mentioned, our responsibility is to make ourselves feel more comfortable. Depending upon who we are, our nervous nature, emotional states, and factors such as environment, we may feel the need to protect ourselves just in case the conflict does turn physical in nature. This is where we introduce the dynamic technique known as the Fence. This technique has been developed over a long period. It is not just a physical movement but has a huge bearing on a conflict. It is built to protect our personal space. The Fence technique utilizes NLP (neurolinguistic programming) to engage with the subconscious mind. Like this chapter, there are stages to this technique as well!

When you combine the use of effective verbal and nonverbal communication, you have the large part of the package. As mentioned in the previous chapter, it has been noted through study that 55 percent of communication is nonverbal and as such covers the physical aspect of the Fence; however, there is still the other 45 percent, which covers the verbal aspect. The same study indicates that 38 percent of total communication incorporates the vocal attributes while the remaining 7 percent are the actual spoken words. It's not what we say; it's how we say it.

If indeed this initial stage is nonphysical in nature, then why put ourselves into a defensive posture? As mentioned earlier it all comes down to our perceived threat as the truth of conflict is in how we perceive it. Stage 2 of conflict is the initiation of physical force. When will that happen? This is an extremely open-ended question as everyone perceives things in different ways. The art of Shoto-Chi teaches the very dynamics of conflict, and over time those that train within this art learn how to emit and read the body language of others as well know the signals they emit themselves. Not only this, the art teaches how to use NLP techniques to implant thoughts and ideas into the brain. Being able to understand and use psychological techniques within conflict is an extremely powerful tool to have.

So let us move on to covering the initial stage of the defensive posture known as the Fence. The Fence in its very definition is "the intention to resolve with authority." It uses a subtle blend of movements that are aimed at relaxing ourselves within conflict but also giving us the optimum positioning should we need it from a conflict turning physical in nature.

For stage 1 of conflict, we initiate the cupped-hand position. The hands are placed lightly cupped in front of the body as indicated in figure 1.

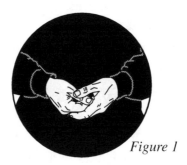

Figure 1

It doesn't matter which hand is on top; it simply needs to feel comfortable and relaxing. Within conflict we are often unaware of the signals we emit. As we start to become more emotional our mind and body start to tense up. The cupped-hand technique is in place to demonstrate a calm approach. By tensing up, therefore potentially making a fist, we are then emitting completely different signals.

In addition to the cupped-hand technique there are also other hand positions, such as the steeple technique. This technique places all the finger tips together pointing outward. This technique is commonly used by those demonstrating a higher intellect. It is a very calm-looking posture; however, without, the calm emotional state to support it, the steeple can emit extreme signals of nervousness and fear. As people start to get nervous, they fidget. Movement within the steeple technique becomes easily visible. Also when tenseness is demonstrated the tips of the figures will lighten significantly as the pressure is increased. So if you are level headed and calm within conflict, then this technique can be very beneficial. If you have a tendency to allow your emotions to guide you, then it may be best to refrain from using it!

The steeple hand is also often seen as a signal of religion; this hand gesture represents prayer but also is used frequently to demonstrate superiority. The steeple effect indicates a confidence or a self-assured attitude. When this gesture is transformed into one of a prayer-like gesture outside of this content, it can make someone seem false, smug, or arrogant. This kind of gesture is also used by someone looking for forgiveness.

Let us now move away from the hand positioning and on to the stance. Many people tend to remain square in their stance. Square indicates that both feet are parallel to each other as shown here in figure 2.

Figure 2

There is nothing wrong with using this positioning during a verbal interaction. The use of the cupped-hands in conjunction with the square stance still provides a calming base. Should we pick up on signals that there is a potential for the conflict turning physical, then this stance becomes a risk. Look at it this way: When looking at someone standing square in front of you, you can see and easily reach 50 percent of them. I state this percent as, without moving, you can only get to the entire front of that person.

If there is evidence of a conflict potentially turning physical, then this is where we introduce the bladed stance as shown in figure 3.

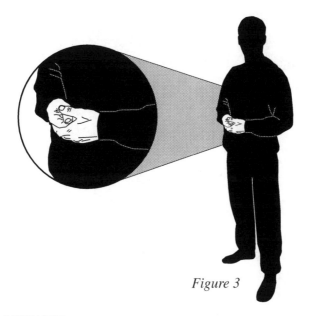

Figure 3

IMPORTANT:

• The relaxed cupped hands demonstrate calmness.

• The relaxed cupped hands help to calm us internally.

• The cupped hands are in a centralized position.

The bladed stance reduces that target area and therefore reduces that predetermined 50 percent. In most cases a person will take the dominant side to the rear. As shown in figure 3, this would indicate the person is predominantly right-handed. This is a result of the brain sending signals to use the strongest side to stabilize ourselves. It is also the side that we need to protect the most and would in turn be used for striking should a conflict turn physical. There are, of course, exceptions to this rule. Over many years of teaching this technique, I have found that those who step back on the opposite leg to their dominant side have tended to not have played many sports while growing up. As a result, the brain has not determined a dominant side with regard to physical movement. This is not always the case, but over the years this theory has proven itself correct at least 95 percent of the time. Think of almost every sport. Does one use a dominant side?

Leaving the hands cupped, we also assist in eliminating a target area—in this case, the lower abdominal region. If we probe even deeper into this position, as one becomes more comfortable and confident in using it, then it helps us to relax. Students of Shoto-Chi have found that the use of the cupped-hand technique in collaboration with the bladed stance sends signals to their brains to calm themselves. As you practice this technique, you will more than likely find the same. Even through this technique is taught in far greater depth within Shoto-Chi, the basic principles still apply to those of you unfamiliar with this technique.

We *teach* others how to *treat* us.

STAGE 2

This second stage describes the change within the conflict to a heightened state. It describes that the conflict has progressed into a physical encounter. This could be due to the defendant's verbal and nonverbal messages not having the desired effect or simply because the aggressor's frame of mind was physical to begin with and there was no stopping it! A conflict can also start from this stage in our mind. Remember, not all conflicts start with verbal interaction. However, there is always a reason for why people do what they do. If someone was to take a conflict directly to the physical stage, we may think it started there, but truly it did not. The person choosing to take the conflict physical had already made a decision. The defendant may not have been aware of this, but something built up to this stage.

This is the most pivotal time within the conflict. It is the key time in which a peaceful resolution can still be achieved or the possibility of the conflict growing into a full-blown physical encounter. In conjunction with the three verbal stages of conflict, we are married up with the Suggestion stage.

We have all heard others say at times that they were taken by surprise. This could well be true if they were unaware of their surroundings or if someone has gone to great lengths to conceal themselves prior to attacking. Stage 1 indicates the initiation of conflict by there being a change in our environment.

Imagine this situation. A man is at the bar of a nightclub. While standing at the bar, he catches the eye of a woman and starts talking to her. She is simply having a polite conversation while waiting for her boyfriend to return from the men's room. As the boyfriend exits the men's room and glances across the room, he notices his girlfriend with an unfamiliar man becoming acquainted! Now the boyfriend happens to have a short fuse! As he walks closer to the pair talking at the bar, his imagination is already running wild. As he gets even closer, he sees the other man gently touch the arm of his girlfriend and they are both laughing. The boyfriend is no longer frustrated; he is now angry. Failing to contain his emotions, he lashes out in anger with a big right hook and floors the man talking to his girlfriend. In the mind of the man that just got floored, that hook came out of nowhere, but it didn't. Now add to the equation that this guy just happened to be a long-time close friend of the girlfriend's family, and now you have a huge misunderstanding. Why?

Simply because the boyfriend, as many others, jumped to a conclusion and did not have the intellect to ask questions. We can certainly make up the balance of this story, but there is no point in doing so. The point has been made. There is always a stage 1.

The most common form of physical attack is pushing. The reason for this is that most conflicts going physical do so out of frustration. Frustration becomes anger, which leads to a more direct attack, such as jabs or hooking punches. If we continue to understanding the dynamic Fence technique, then we learn how to use this to our advantage when understanding emotional impact. Let us look at pushing, for example. There is a high probability that, if someone pushes once, they will do so a second time, especially if they got the desired result the first time. We can also send subconscious messages to the brain to ensure that the second push is where we want it to be. That's right, I'm talking about getting inside the head of the aggressor and planting a seed of deception. Their mind sees an avenue of opportunity but does not understand that we suggested the idea.

Let me explain some more.

During a heated discussion the frustrated party decides to push. They use both hands and push against the chest of the person in front of them. As the person takes a step back to stabilize himself, the aggressor then pushes again. The aggressor doesn't push using two hands this time but only one. This time they only push the shoulder closest to them. Why?

Simply put, it was the most convenient and simplest access point when the person stepped back, therefore blading their stance and more specifically their shoulders. The aggressor's brain picked up on signals and acted upon it within a split second. As defendants we can also manipulate our body language to send out similar signals.

The reality of accurately defending an initial push is extremely low unless a full defensive posture is implemented; however, effectively defending against the follow-up is extremely high. The main reason is that we can effectively position ourselves to deal with the second push, knowing the signals we are emitting. If we were to step back in a square stance with square shoulders, then the likelihood of an identical push is extremely high, but by stepping back bladed, the chances are dramatically reduced. This is a solely covering the footwork and shoulders, let alone the arm and hand gestures!

As you have now started to understand, there is so much more to effective and realistic self-defense. We can be proactive in our approach versus taking the traditional reactive approach. By learning effective personal space management skills inclusive of verbal and nonverbal, we are in a wonderful position to resolve conflict even if, as stated in this stage, the conflict has a physical element to it. When someone is acting out of frustration, we can help them to help themselves.

I remember a personal experience back in the late 1990s. At the time, I was working at a local pub in my hometown in England as a doorman/bouncer. This particular night started like many others. I greeted many as they came into the pub, had some friendly banter, and turned away a few that had started to drink way too early!

One of my own students was also having a night out with friends. He had recently had a breakup with a girlfriend, and like many breakups, it wasn't the prettiest.

A local man around the same age as my student but renowned for causing trouble had a personal grudge against him as a result of the breakup. He decided to come down to the pub with the intention of fighting. Luckily he decided to attempt to enter the pub through the door I was covering. As he approached the door with a face like thunder and fists clenched, it was plain to see things were not going to go well should he enter. Now at this time, I wasn't aware of the issues previously mentioned. As he approached, I politely stopped him. I asked him if he was okay, and through his use of colorful metaphors, it was clear to see that he was not.

He wasn't frustrated at this time. He was beyond frustration, even anger. He was more bordering on hatred, which is never a good place to be. He attempted to force his way past me a couple of times without success. Upon redirecting him a few feet from the building, I was able to reengage verbally. I asked open-ended questions and discovered what was on his mind. Once he informed me of his intentions, I had to inform him that he wouldn't be entering the establishment. At this time he drew a blade. The owner of the establishment was keeping a close eye on things and informed me through my ear piece that he would be calling the authorities. I asked him not to and that I would handle it. Due to his trust in my ability to do the job, he did not make the call.

Upon defusing the knife situation through effective authoritative techniques, I was able to talk him down and convince him to leave, which he did. The following night he came back. He had slept off the previous night and was much calmer. He took the opportunity to apologize, and we never had another encounter of the hostile kind again. He respected the fact that I did not use excessive force or involve the authorities.

Had I not been skilled in this area, things would have turned out very differently. Had I decided to react and solely use my physical skill set, then the result would have been extremely different. I'm not talking about him not entering the establishment; I'm talking about the mutual respect and peaceful outcome by one person within the conflict, looking out for the best interest of all involved.

If you have the opportunity to resolve a conflict without the use of excessive force or ideally no force at all, then that approach should be adopted. At that particular moment in history and in conjunction with the second stage of physical conflict, we demonstrate that even when a conflict becomes physical, there is still a chance to resolve peacefully in the best interest of all parties.

Let us now look at the continuation of the Fence technique as started in stage 1. We initially covered the use of the cupped hand while in either a square or ideally bladed stance. As we progress with this dynamic technique, we introduce the shift in hand positioning from cupped to actual Fence.

Introducing the front hand of the Fence indicates that there is a perceived threat to our personal space. This should be supported with effective verbal communication as covered in previous chapters. With no change to the positioning of the feet, raise the front hand into position. The front hand should be brought into position using a rolling technique from the inside. This way the palm is gradually introduced and by doing so demonstrates calmness. The rolling method should come directly from the cupped hands in a side-to-side motion versus from the bottom up. Bringing the front hand up from the bottom produces more of a flicking technique and does not send the same signals to the brain as the rolling method. The speed and fluency in which this is carried out is also extremely important. The slower the movement, the calmer demeanor it demonstrates. Obviously at times, due to the aggressor's demeanor, we may need to speed up the process. If we have the opportunity, therefore time, to use slower movement, then we should. Aggressors are looking for us to panic, to act without confidence. Calmness is very unsettling to an aggressor.

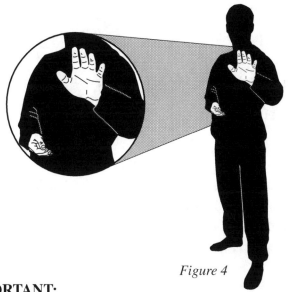

Figure 4

IMPORTANT:

• The palm *must* be clearly visible to the person it is facing as this represents the intention to *resolve*.

• The palm *must* be centered and relaxed with *no* curling of the fingers. The fingers *must* be slightly parted as this demonstrates a relaxed demeanor.

• Do *not* block the mouth as this sends negative signals to the person you are facing. You want to ensure the aggressor has a clean line of sight to your mouth.

• The height of the *front* hand is therefore adjustable based upon the height of the person it is facing.

• Keep all motions smooth. Sudden or sharp movements demonstrate tension.

From this position we have now reduced that initial 50 percent strike area when standing square to more like 20 percent. The abdominal region is still slightly open, but like the head and legs, we are a very small movement away from protecting them. This percentage drops to 10 percent by introducing the rear hand as the abdominal area is now protected.

This brings us to the final stage of the Fence—well, for basic understanding of it, that is! The final stage introduces the use of the rear hand. This hand is also known as the communicator. When needed we use this hand to support our verbal without compromising the defensive front hand.

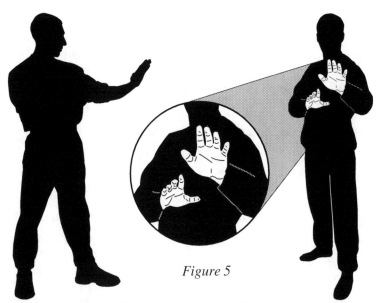

Figure 5

The rear hand has the palm slightly turned down.

The reason for this is that a downward-facing palm represents authority but also allows for the palms to be visible. This engages with the brain far better than having the palm out of sight as nonvisible hands are a verbal cue toward deception. We are looking to resolve and in order to do so we want to appear open. As also mentioned this rear hand is used to communicate nonverbal messages, such as helping to calm down by gently raising and lowering the hand in a "patting" style movement.

IMPORTANT:

• The palms *must* be clearly visible to the person it is facing.

• The rear palm is to face slightly downward.

• This represents *authority.*

• The back hand protects the midsection of the body.

• The palms *must* be relaxed with *no* curling of the fingers.

• The fingers *must* be slightly parted.

• Only the *back* hand does the nonverbal communication.

• Keep all motions smooth. Sudden or sharp moves demonstrate tension.

Should a counter strike be required, then it should be one that allows you the opportunity for space and time to verbally communicate one final time. Any counter strike deemed necessary by the defendant must be in conjunction with the appropriate laws on self-defense. A defendant can be prosecuted if a counter strike is proven to be used with intent or excessive force. At this point the aggressor should be given the choice to back down. This can be done in numerous ways using a variety of verbal techniques. You don't actually have to say "Make the right choice" or "Make a good choice," although these can work! Your objective is to let the aggressor know that you would prefer a peaceful resolution versus physical. The idea is to plant a seed in their mind that assists them to make a choice, knowing full well that the choice to continue physically may not be in their best interest.

Giving a choice and providing options pass the ownership to the aggressor. They must then choose fight or flight, knowing that they run the risk of pursuing a physical conflict with someone that has a higher level of intelligence and skill set than they may have originally anticipated.

With the physical steps of the basic Fence completed, we now need to focus on our facial expression.

Smiling is not recommended when looking to resolve with authority. It sends out conflicting messages in conjunction with the nonverbal communication signals. Keep an assertive facial expression that shows little or no emotion. This, when supported with the effective use of assertive body language, can become very unsettling for the aggressor. Making the aggressor feel uncomfortable means you are starting to get inside their mind, which can possibly lead to their self-doubt. This is an assertive place to be and provides us with an incredible opportunity to resolve the conflict without any further physical interaction.

Now, there is obviously the other argument that humor can work to resolve conflict. I do not disagree with this when a conflict is in the earlier stages. In fact humor can be of great benefit and should be used whenever possible. But do not replace the thought that just because you are good with humor, it means you are good at resolving conflict. Humor is used more often than not within conflict. The reality is that, in most cases, humor is an unconscious defense mechanism. However, when a conflict reaches intense levels, humor should be set aside. As we move into stage 3 of physical conflict, we shall understand this even more.

SUMMARY OF STEPS:

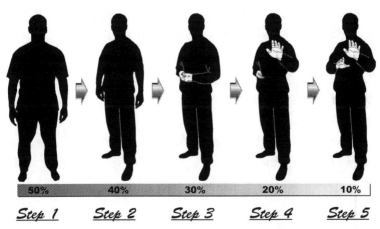

50%	40%	30%	20%	10%
Step 1	*Step 2*	*Step 3*	*Step 4*	*Step 5*

The speed in which the transitions happen is conflict specific. Most conflicts will not even warrant the use of the Fence in regards to steps 4 and 5. As indicated earlier, it is unwise to stay square to a possible physical threat. As soon as there is a perceived threat to our personal space, we should be positioning ourselves into a bladed stance as shown in steps 2 and 3. Under each silhouette there is a percentage scale that shows the threat assessment using the Fence. It starts at 50 percent as the entire front of the body is open to physical assault.

STAGE 3

By this point within a conflict, hopefully things would have been resolved in a peaceful manner. If not, then it means that the aggressor has chosen to ignore your verbal and nonverbal messages and continue the conflict in a physical manner. This is with the intent to cause serious bodily harm. It states that your method of resolution was of no interest to the aggressor and that they decided to throw caution to the wind!

With a definite perceived threat to one's personal space, it is now essential that we take authoritative control of the conflict in both verbal and nonverbal aspects. In this case our verbal must remain calm yet extremely authoritative in order to support the full use of the Fence.

An authoritative context must now be introduced to relay the message of the intention to resolve with authority. *But be ready!*

Authoritative terminology can also bring about rebellion as aggressive personalities do not like others taking control. In stating this, they may also respect it as you are mirroring part of their own personality. The common statement for this is "We look for in others what we see in ourselves"—a true statement for the most part.

It goes without saying that the nonverbal aspect of the communication must also be authoritative in order to support the verbal message. Words and phrases such as "Back off, "Step back," "Back down," or "Walk away" are all authoritative. Alternative phrasing may include "Seriously!" "Not a good move," or "I seriously do not recommend you continue this physical." Such alternative phrasing displays calmness, confidence, and intelligence. The message here is to provide you with an idea. We all use different phrasing, and I'm confident that you can put phrasing together that works for you and stays true to the goal of resolution at the juncture.

When at this stage of conflict there are a few words and phrases that offer too much respect and should therefore not be used. Words such as "Please" or "Sorry" offer too much respect. Try to refrain from using them. Phrases or expressions such as "Thank you" should be exchanged with those that express a higher level of intelligence, such as "I appreciate that." In addition to the choice of words and phrases that we should be cognizant of using, there are also a few other things to remember. Never repeat yourself—this demonstrates the inability to follow through. Also remember, for a conflict to turn physical, they need to start it. Do not allow yourself to get baited in to physical conflict. Be sure that if a conflict is to go into the final stages of physicality, then it does so on your terms.

Now you inform them that they made the wrong choice. The responsibility of the defendant is to resolve the conflict in a swift and timely manner using the appropriate defense and counter-striking techniques. Remember to respond in conjunction with the law by the use of necessary force. At this time our thought process needs to be forward thinking. A defensive-thinking mentality at this stage is detrimental to ending the conflict. Think of a light switch. At the moment of a conflict progressing to stage 3, that light needs to go on. The mind needs to be focused but must also remain calm. The aggressor has made a decision to harm you, and you must make the decision to end the conflict.

There is *no* stage 4.

Stages 2 and 3 focus on the physical side of conflict. This is not easy, because it is real. It is not training or competition fighting. It is not martial-art-style sparring and there are no rules. It is very real. It is a moment that even experienced martial artists have been known to freeze. Why? Because there is a huge difference between martial arts training and real-life conflict. Real-life conflict involves real emotions, real environments, and in many cases hidden agendas.

There is no question that training in most forms of martial arts can be of true benefit when it comes to building character, self-confidence, and self-control. But as in most areas of learning, it comes down to those who teach these arts and those that choose to learn. There are thousands of truly exceptional instructors in the world teaching a variety of arts. But it is your choice as to what you feel you would benefit from. Be sure to research styles/systems, and make sure that the instructors are indeed qualified to teach what they claim to teach. Just because someone may be a great martial artist doesn't make them a great instructor. There is a huge difference between training and teaching. Find an instructor that compliments you—an instructor that lives and teaches by a strong code of ethics and an instructor that believes in you more than the success of their club.

In order to find the right art/system for you, ask yourself the following questions:

Am I looking for traditional structure and discipline?
Is my goal to work through belts?
Do I want competitions?
Am I looking to learn how to compete or defend?
Do I want to learn how to fight or defend?

These questions and more can help to narrow down the right art for you. If you are looking to learn groundwork, then choose something like jujitsu. If it is a traditional discipline you seek, then learn karate. Interested in weapons training? Now there are also many out there for that.

Those of us that have been in the martial arts for many years and have made the conscious choice to grow within the arts have usually learnt more than a few different disciplines.

In order to grow we need to experience different things. Never limit the mind to one system, unless that system is not governed by structure, therefore having the ability to evolve itself.

As the great Bruce Lee once said, "Be like water, my friend."

Also keep in mind that, in order to learn effective self-defense, one does not have to learn martial arts as such. There are some extremely effective and realistic programs out there that focus solely on teaching self-awareness and self-defense. One such program and one that I fully endorse is available through SAFE International Inc. The managing director of SAFE, Chris Roberts, has done an amazing job of putting together a self-defense program that focuses on gross motor skills. It does not teach martial arts techniques, and the program is extremely humorous at the same time. The humor also helps those that participate to retain the information taught. The programs are aimed at those that want to learn self-defense without undertaking years of martial arts training and thousands of dollars.

Obviously in conjunction with this, Shoto-Chi is built around conflict resolution and offers an extremely in-depth approach to conflict resolution. This book just skims the surface of my art.

Conflict Resolution
Tip of Day!

Understand the nature of the conflict. Is it based upon structure, is it situational, or is it personality driven? Once you understand this, you can now start to resolve. How do we do this? Ask open-ended questions with a calm and welcoming tone. Remember, you are seeking to resolve and not continue. Resolving conflict means allowing all parties to feel good about the result.

Negotiating

Words can be your most powerful tool or your worst weapon.

As explained in the chapter "Understanding Conflict," the art of Shoto-Chi teaches by the five principal philosophies. The second of which is "Remember, words can never harm you." Words can only harm you if you allow them to. Remember to view this principal philosophy in a positive light. Most importantly remember to not allow words to affect you in your decision making and also never to use words to attack others.

Conflict negotiating requires finding a common ground in which to agree upon. This could be in many different ways. Those life-changing decisions should be based upon fact, not emotions. Each party should understand how and why the decision has been made, reminding each other of the consensus goal. When debating, ensure that there is a clear line for communication, verbal and nonverbal. Whenever possible, remove distractions in order to focus on the task at hand. But remember, it is not only a case of what you say; it's also how you say it.

Of course you have feelings and are fully entitled to reasonably voice those feelings in a constructive manner, but you should not be childish, abusive, or immature in your approach to the conflict negotiations. There will no doubt be disagreements along the way; the real questions is, do you go into the negotiations seeking resolution or a continuation to the conflict? Think positively toward your goal.

> ## "POSITIVE INPUT
> ### PRODUCES
> ### POSITIVE OUTPUT"

Do not look at it as a competition but as a partnership whereby the needs of the people involved are met.

Here are a few rules of effective negotiating:

• First and foremost, know your objectives.
What is it you are trying to accomplish? Ensure that all parties know the common goal. Most people do not want to be in conflict, so using that as an opener works fairly well!

• Understand the nature of the conflict. Is it based upon structure, is it situational, or is it personality driven?
Know and understand the very dynamics of the conflict. Understanding this helps to focus on the task at hand. You may need to ask some effective and open-ended questions to figure this out at times.

• Remain in control of your calmness and emotions.
This is the first of the five Shoto-Chi principal philosophies and indicates the importance of calmness. It is pretty difficult to resolve conflict when all involved are running at

a heightened emotional state. Calmness allows us to focus and inject the much-needed logic.

• Never personalize the dispute.
In order to find resolution, we have to remove the personal aspect and focus on the facts. Focus on what, not who. Personalizing a conflict can never bring about a resolution that makes everyone involved feel good about themselves.

• Keep it relevant and real.
It is easy when in conflict to become side-railed. The most common and destructive means of doing this is to bring up the past. As mentioned earlier in this book, there is no place for the past. Keep on track to resolution. Focus on the relevancy of the topic to the conflict and keep it real.

• Understand the message and disregard the emotions.
Now this is a tough one. We spent time early on in this book discussing the power of emotions within conflict and how we need to take them into account. So now you see me mention that we should disregard the emotions. The meaning of this is to understand the message within the emotion. Emotions are a reaction to an event; therefore, understanding what caused the emotion is far more important than the emotion itself.

• Don't compete but compromise instead.
Conflict resolution shouldn't be about the need to be right; it should be about the resolution of the conflict. When there are more than two people within the conflict, then competing doesn't provide equality. Search for the compromise that

works in the best interests of all involved.

• Accept your part of the responsibility.
Now this is an interesting statement to make and something many people find hard to swallow. In so many cases people only want to see the other at fault. This is one of the main reasons for so many failed relationships. When working your way through conflict negotiating, therefore seeking resolution, it is important to look at all aspects of the conflict. Being the calm one and the one looking to resolve things, you can logically analyze things to see what part all parties played in the conflict. In many cases you will find that, in some strange way, we all play a part. Remember that conflict is all about perception!

• Distribute the credit.
This is the final and most critical step to resolving the conflict. It is of paramount importance that the conflict comes to a resolute state with all parties feeling good about the outcome. Sure, you may have been the guiding light toward resolving the conflict, but once you've got things calmed down, all within the conflict resolution process joined in. Giving each other that pat on the back or hug makes everyone feel they played their part, and they did.

There are many methods of negotiating within conflict resolution. It all comes down to you and your personal approach. There is the avoidance method, which includes a completely unassertive and uncooperative approach. It is uncooperative because we do not engage at all in the conflict but run as far away from it as possible. We completely downplay the situation to the point of not acknowledging that a conflict even exists. Our goal with this strategy is to remain neutral at all costs and avoid any confrontation. This approach demonstrates an extremely low level of self-confidence. Most people that use this approach usually have many internal conflicts, hence the reason for shying away from conflict but also not realizing they are in the biggest conflict of them all.

In addition to the avoidance method, there is also the accommodating approach. This involves using an unassertive yet cooperative approach, allowing the other person to get their way. It certainly smoothes over the conflict very quickly but brings about an artificial conclusion as you have not found personal resolution; therefore, the conflict has only been resolved in the best interest of the other party. This approach creates a false reality and often leads us down a path of resentment. Similar to the avoidance method, it is the result of low self-esteem. Those that use this approach take the world on the shoulders in the hope of a quieter life but are unhappy in the process.

As we progress in methodology of negotiating tactics, we next come to those that seek the compromise. Those that adopt this approach have struck a fine balance between avoidance and cooperation. They make it their goal to not run away from conflict but to face it head-on with the sole intention of finding a peaceful resolution for everyone involved. Their goal, however, is sometimes a little shortsighted as they are more concerned with finding an acceptable solution for those involved versus the complete solution. What happens in these cases is as much as the conflict is resolved at the time, it is usually a temporary resolution and the core problem still needs to be resolved. As a result of this, the conflict quite often reappears at a later date.

Stepping up the ladder of negotiating techniques, we then look at resolution as a form of competition. Those that adopt this approach take command through authoritative actions. They take control with an assertive approach but are less cooperative toward finding a solution in the best interest of all involved. They don't really work in favor of the collective harmony than for their own personal satisfaction. They will fight their way to the finish line in order to win the conflict, forcing things to a conclusion that suits their needs and they have no problems stamping their authority over the situation. This leads to the other party feeling less than equal.

With some of the less-than-ideal methods of negotiating conflict resolution out of the way, we can now look at the most ideal approach. The better approach that takes into consideration of the needs of all involved parties yet also seeks a permanent solution is something that looks to resolve through a collaborative approach. These people enjoy the problem-solving aspect of resolving conflict. Even though they are part of the conflict, they also thrive on resolving it. In order to do so, they take the lead through a respectful but assertive manner. They look to start the healing process by reaching out in the hope that the other party will accept their approach toward finding a resolution that suits all involved. Their priority and focus is seeking harmony by working though the differences in perception to achieve the optimum result of resolution. This is the win-win approach whereby all parties achieve what is best for them as individuals as well the relationship between those within the conflict—working together to find a place of harmony.

How a dispute ends is critical to its lasting success. Allow each other to retreat with dignity and respect, knowing that a hand has been reached out. We all require some guidance in our lives from time to time. That may come from one another or an outside source. Remember what you set out to achieve, and no matter how small the steps may seem, they will lead you in the right direction.

Acknowledge the problem, make the choice to want to fix it, then work together to find the solution.

Conflict Resolution
Tip of Day!

*Make a conscious choice to use words as a tool
and not as a weapon. Choose your words carefully
so they become a welcomed addition to resolving
the conflict, but remember that conflict doesn't
always have to be with another. Keep your own
self-talk free of negativity!*

About The Author

Rob Norton's reason for creating Shoto-Chi was simple. He wanted to develop an art that would constantly evolve. An art that had no restriction or boundaries set by outside forces. An art that could be taught to every individual's needs and requirements and helps people to get the most out of life.

Developing and teaching Shoto-Chi is a true passion for the founder, Robert James Norton, PhD. In his own words, "It is an art that is part of my core being."

He has been involved with martial arts since a young age, starting in Shotokan karate. He achieved first-degree black belt at the age of fifteen but was teaching others from the age of thirteen under the guidance of his sensei, Barry Lewis. He also obtained his instructor's license in 1989. By the age of seventeen he had started to develop the foundations of Shoto-Chi while studying at university. In 1990 he opened up his first club in his hometown in England. Developing a new martial art at such a young age brought about many challenges due to his age, but he was determined to overcome adversity and teach what he was developing.

His vision was finally recognized in 1999 when he was officially awarded the title of Master. He proved to the governing body for martial arts in the UK that his art was truly unique, and they recognized him as a true founder.

Rob Norton has spent many years studying human behavior. He has and continues to study conflict psychology. He worked as a bouncer/doorman for many years and also trained in close protection. His passion is teaching his art and making a positive impact in the lives of others. Teaching his art has brought him many rewards over the years. The greatest of which has been seeing his students gain a greater level of self-confidence and propel themselves forward in life.

His goal with teaching Shoto-Chi is to help people gain a greater understanding of conflict resolution from a realistic perspective—to show people that you have to *behave your way to success* in order to get the right results.

In 2013 Rob Norton was officially awarded Grand Master status while having Shoto-Chi recognized within the United

States of America. In this same year he also obtained his PhD in martial science, which helped to inspire him to publish this, his first book. Rob Norton was also inducted into the US Martial Arts Hall of Fame in 2013 for International Founder of the Year.

Today he resides in Canada with his family and continues to teach and develop his art. His method of teaching is certainly unique and he proves that you can *create, achieve, and live your goals*.

Ethics • Integrity • Respect

www.shoto-chi.com

References

Wikipedia (Personality types)

Dimitrius, J., and M. Mazzarella. Reading People. New York: Ballantine, 1999.

Pease, A., and B. Pease. The Definitive Book of Body Language. New York: Bantam Dell, 2006.

Rohm, R., and J. A. Cross. You've Got Style, 2nd ed. Atlanta: Personality Insights, 2001.

While every care is taken to prevent copyrighted images from being featured without permission, if you own the copyright to an image and would like it removed, please contact us and we will do so immediately.